SKIING TO WIN

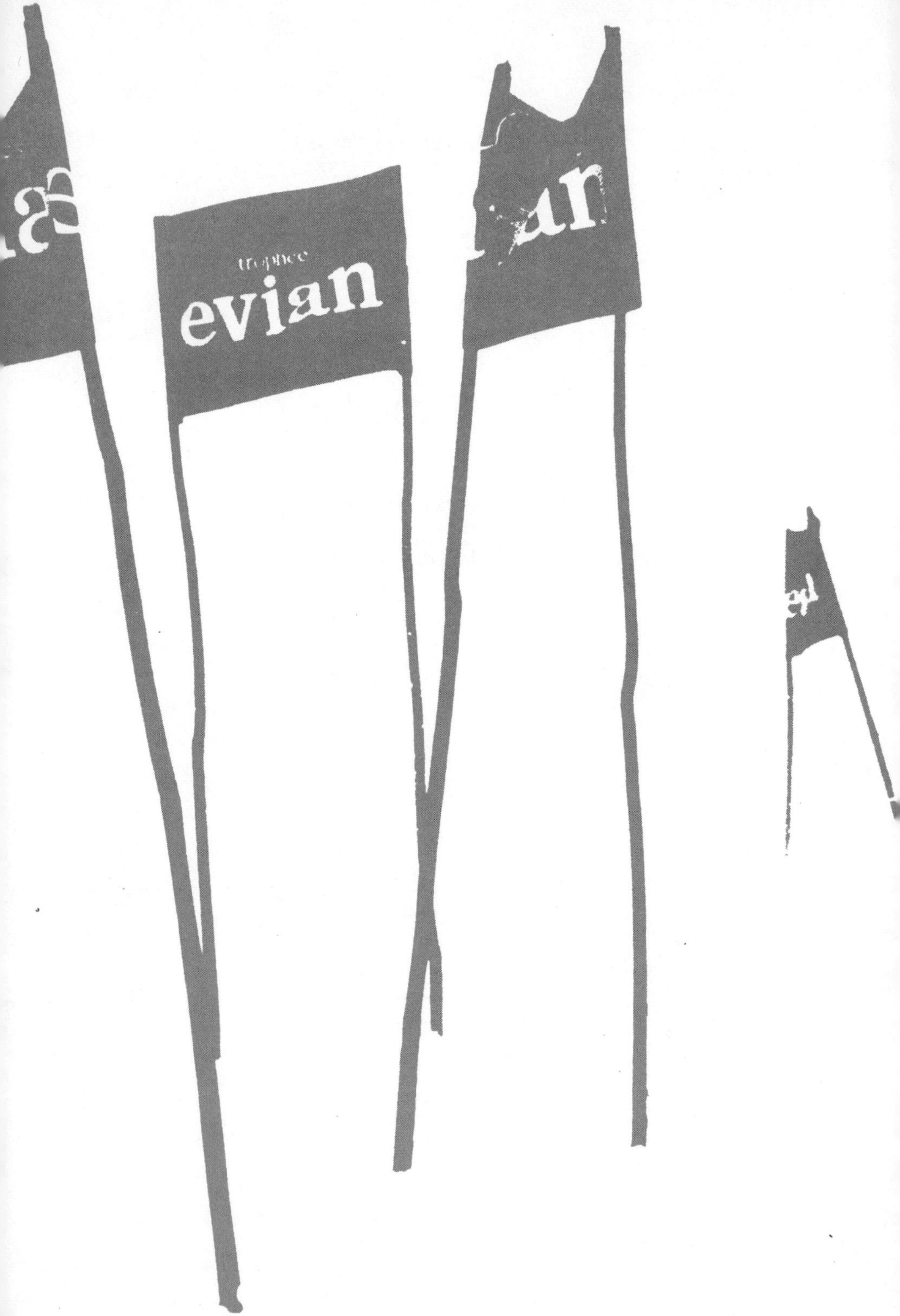
trophee
evian

SKIING TO WIN

HARVEY EDWARDS

Illustrated with photographs

Harcourt Brace Jovanovich, Inc.
New York

Library of Congress Cataloging in Publication Data

Edwards, Harvey.
Skiing to win.

SUMMARY: Describes major competition skiing events
throughout the world including biographies of
international skiing champions and a special section
on ski touring.
1. Ski racing—Biography—Juvenile literature.
2. Cross-country skiing—Juvenile literature.
[1. Ski racing—Biography. 2. Cross-country skiing]
I. Title.
GV854.2.A1E37   796.9′3′0922 [920]   73-5239
ISBN 0-15-275400-8

Frontispiece based on a photograph by Harvey Edwards

This book is dedicated to my mother who,

for the past fifteen years,

has been trying to figure out what I have been doing

ACKNOWLEDGMENTS

Editors John Fry of *Ski Magazine,* Doug Pfeiffer and Al Greenberg of *Skiing,* and Bob Ottum of *Sports Illustrated* made available back files of their magazines. With their permission, for which I am very grateful, I have quoted freely from articles that appeared therein.

Over the years, Mike Brady's excellent book, *Nordic Touring and Cross-Country Skiing* (Dreyers Forlag, Oslo) and John Caldwell's *Cross-Country Ski Book* (Stephen Greene Press, Brattleboro, Vermont) helped introduce me to cross-country skiing. In addition Mr. Brady kindly supplied background material on Sixten Jernberg and John Bower for the cross-country chapter; but, as in all the other material, I am responsible for its interpretation.

I would also like to thank the many past and present members and coaches of the United States Alpine and Nordic ski teams, many of whom I have known for many years, for their patience during interviews and at critical moments during the competition seasons. Throughout this book, I have used material obtained through taped interviews and informal discussions with Bob Beattie, Gordie Eaton, Willy Schaeffler, Henry Tauber, Al Merrill, Tom Kelly, Hans Peter Rohr, Johnny Caldwell, John Balfanz, and Marty Hall, among the U.S. ski coaches, past and present; Bobby Cochran, Mike Lafferty, Don Rowles, Eric Poulsen, Tim Caldwell,

Nancy Greene, Suzy Corrock, Marilyn and Barbara Ann Cochran, Cindy Nelson, and Martha Rockwell, among the racers. Without their cooperation, this book could never have been written.

In recounting the story of Léon Zwingelstein in the ski touring chapter, I relied on Jacques Dieterlen's *Le Chemineau de la Montagne* (Flammarion, Paris).

Many other writers and journalists, too numerous to mention, have been helpful either through personal contact or through reading their books and articles. In particular, I would like to thank Michel Clare for permission to quote from his book, *Jean-Claude Killy,* Hachette, Paris, 1968; and Nancy Greene for permission to quote from her autobiography, *Nancy Greene,* published by the General Publishing Company, Limited, Don Mills, Ontario, 1968.

CONTENTS

SKIING TO WIN

1
THE BEST IN THE WORLD

Men and women began to ski about 4,000 years ago, but because people have always wanted to go faster and better and prove their ability by measuring themselves against others, ski racing probably began at the same time. Today there are two types of competitive skiing: Nordic, in which the major events are cross-country and jumping, and Alpine, consisting of the downhill and slalom. In the downhill, racers ski from the top to the bottom of a prescribed course by the shortest possible route; in slalom races, the object is to ski through a series of gates that are set up so that they test the maneuvering ability of the skier. In both events, skiers race against the clock, with the shortest time determining the winner.

Modern Alpine ski racing started with what are now generally regarded as the ski classics. For men these are: the Hahnenkamm ski meeting at Kitzbühel, Austria; the Lauberhorn races at Wengen, Switzerland; the Grand Prix de Megève, France; and the Arlberg-Kandahar, which is held in four resorts—St. Anton, Austria; Mürren, Switzerland; Sestriere, Italy; and Chamonix, France. Aside from the Kandahar, which is a women's race as well, the women's classics are held at Grindelwald, Switzerland; St. Gervais, France; and Schruns or Bad Gastein, Austria.

Many ski racers to whom I have talked have indicated that, purely from a racing standpoint, they would prefer to win the classic races than either the World Ski Championships or the Olympic Games. The Englishman Sir Arnold Lunn created the Kandahar with the Austrian Hannes Schneider back in 1928, and the Lauberhorn and Hahnenkamm races were founded a few years later. Aside from war or no-snow years, these races have been held ever since. The classic ski races have a certain undeniable tradition that all racers respect. Although the Olympic and world championship races can be held anywhere in the world, the classic races are held in areas where the *pistes* or racing tracks are extremely challenging, demanding tremendous skills, concentration, and poise. The classics are proven events, the true test of a ski racer's mettle. Add to the above reasons the fact that as many as 20,000 spectators turn out for these annual events and you have some idea of the pressure that can be on an international class racer when he steps into the starting gate at Kitzbühel, Wengen, or St. Gervais.

The Olympic Games are held every four years and the World Ski Championships every two years. Actually, the Olympic Games are considered the World Championships by the Fédération Internationale de Ski or the FIS, which controls amateur ski racing all over the world. Therefore, in Olympic years the games serve as the World Championships. The FIS awards a combined medal at the Olympic Games, which is the result of a calculation of points based on best placings in the downhill, slalom, and giant slalom. Thus, in 1970 America's Billy Kidd placed high enough in the three events to win the combined at Val Gardena. He was given a gold medal as the best all-around skier during the World Championships. Combined awards are also given in the classic ski races and in many other races as well.

When starting an Olympic or World Championship season, a different kind of pressure is on a racer's shoulders than during the classic events. Often racers will build up to the Olympic Games, that is, pace their season in such a way as to be in peak form during the ten-day period when the championships are held. If an amateur wins an Olympic and/or a FIS medal, his financial future is secure. In all likelihood, he will eventually be marketing his name and reputation.

The World Cup, which should not be confused with the World Championships, was founded in 1966 at Portillo, Chile. The purpose of the World Cup is to select the *season's* best overall performer among the men and women racers. Although the rules have often been changed, in general the way the best skiers in the world are selected is as follows: Before the season begins, certain races are designated World Cup events, which means that in them a racer can win World Cup points if he places among the first ten finishers in the slalom, giant slalom, or downhill, however the case may be. First place receives twenty-five points, second place twenty, third place fifteen, and so on; and a certain maximum number of points is possible in each specialty. After the final World Cup event of the season, the World Cup is awarded to the man and woman skier whose total number of points in the three events is the highest, while additional awards are given to racers with the most points in each event.

To sum up, the Alpine classics are ski racing's most highly esteemed events, at least by the racers and by the knowing public. The Olympics and World Championships give prestige awards to racers who are in peak condition during the championship events, but the World Cup is an annual overall award to racers who have succeeded in maintaining top form throughout the four-month-long competition season.

These then are the events, trophies, and honors that can be won while a ski racer is still a so-called amateur racer. In fact, many of today's amateur racers, once they reach the top levels of international competition, could not by any stretch of the imagination be considered amateurs. This is particularly true of the European racers who are paid by their ski federations and/or under the table by ski equipment manufacturers and are supported by subsidies from their governments. Up until 1973 if American racers were paid at all, they were paid badly. The best ones received somewhere in the neighborhood of $250 per month. In my opinion, if they are to compete successfully in the big time, they should be paid and paid well, mainly because of the time and devotion that is necessary to develop into a top-rate racer and the dangers that are involved. One of the things that this book demonstrates is that for every racer who becomes a national team member, there are probably 10,000 who, for one reason or another, do not make it. If Americans are to stay in the game, those who do make it must be supported by more than scars, trophies, and kind words—even if this means a break with the Olympic movement. In any event, the Winter Olympics cannot continue much longer unless the rules are changed and there is a return to a more realistic and honest view based on the needs of today's racers.

☆　☆　☆

He was born in Kitzbühel, Austria, on Birchlstrasse 10 in 1936. From the window of the house he could see the Hahnenkamm cable car and one of the most challenging downhill *pistes* in all the world—the Streif. He started skiing when he was two years old, and by the time he was six he had already side-slipped down the Streif on skis. Small for his age, he wanted to go far and fast. One day he skied down the Streif eleven times, and an older boy told him, "That's more vertical drop than from the top of Mount Everest to the sea." The young skier did not know that Mount Everest was the highest mountain in the world, but he was too proud to say so.

He gave all his free time to skiing. He startled other skiers by descending chutes and steep faces at breakneck speed. His clothing was dark except for a white stocking cap pulled over his dark hair. When he skidded to a stop, his dark brown eyes gleamed and his white teeth flashed in the soft Austrian winter sun. A black angel! Who was he? "Toni Sailer," the ski teacher said. "Just one of the local boys." Little did they know that Toni Sailer's calm personality and flashing speed were destined to make Kitzbühel the most famous ski town in Austria, perhaps in all the world.

Toni won his first race—a downhill and a jump—when he was eleven years old. His prize: two Austrian sausages. On Sundays he sang in the church choir, and he often helped his father, the town tinsmith, install gutters on the roofs of the Kitzbühel chalets. Standing up there, Toni gazed out at the mountains and imagined himself making tracks on their white faces and in the chutes where the snow was eternal.

The idol of all the boys from Kitzbühel was Christian Pravda, the champion of the local ski club and one of the finest skiers Austria has ever produced. When he was fifteen, Toni beat Pravda in a giant slalom race. Toni Sailer's name made headlines in the Austrian papers, but that was just the beginning. In 1950, 1951, and 1952 he won the Austrian Junior Championships. Then he broke a leg in a bad fall, missed the entire 1953 season, and the following year still was not in top shape. By 1955, he had filled out and grown: 180 pounds, almost six feet tall. That year he won the coveted Lauberhorn race at Wengen, Switzerland, the downhill and combined at Megève, France, and he set the downhill record on the Cortina, Italy, *piste,* which was to be used the following year for the Olympic Games.

By 1956—an Olympic year—Toni Sailer was ready. Before the games he won five races including the Lauberhorn and the Hahnenkamm at Kitzbühel. Race fever ran high in Austria, where skiing was the unofficial national sport. There was no television coverage of ski races at that time, and on race days all of Austria stopped work. Those who could traveled miles to races over bad roads, and thousands of others listened to race accounts on the radio. How would the Black Angel do under the pressure of the Olympic Games, everyone asked. The Austrian ski team, with its super star Toni Sailer, was the greatest in the world. The Olympics would prove it. In February, the Austrian crowds flocked across the border to Cortina, Italy. They crowded into hotel rooms and guesthouses; they jammed into the cafés and restaurants where talk revolved around the question: How would the team do? Would Toni stand up under the pressure?

Toni didn't disappoint them. In the giant slalom he beat teammate Anderl Molterer by an amazing 6.2 seconds, and he took the slalom gold medal away from the American-trained Japanese skier Chiharu Igaya by a comfortable four-second margin.

The downhill, though, promised to be another story. The night before the race a snowstorm raged. Around midnight the wind blew the storm deeper into the Alps, the stars came out, and the cold set in. The following morning the temperature was ten degrees below zero, and the wind was furiously strong. It blew snow off the crests around Cortina, and the powder built up on the *piste.* In those days, downhill tracks were not as carefully groomed as they are today. If they had them at all, racers wore light-weight leather helmets, but they did not have safety bindings. In those days, however, they had more liberty to choose their "line" of descent, but for many of the racers the downhill was interminable: two miles long and 3,000 feet of vertical nightmare. The Faloria course was tricky and dangerous. One by one the racers from twenty-seven nations plunged off the start. The bumps (called moguls) were huge, between them were slabs of blue ice and soft snow, and off to the sides were unprotected rocks. Out of seventy-five racers who started, only forty-seven finished and only seventeen did not fall.

Ten minutes before his start time, Toni Sailer tied on bib number 14 and began to warm up by jumping up and down on his skis and doing deep knee bends. Suddenly, the bitter cold caused one of Toni's leather thongs to snap. Friends rushed around him. His coach said, "No, no, Toni, don't be nervous." Toni was calm, almost serene, just as he always was before a big race. He was concentrating and thinking: "I am listening to the times. I set the record before in 2:26, and the best time now is 2:59. I am thinking it is too much: 30 seconds' difference. I don't know where I can lose 30 seconds." The coach, too nervous to replace the binding himself, handed Toni a leather thong. Toni slipped off his gloves, calmly tied the thong through his binding rings, moved to the start, and pushed off.

One hundred and eighty pounds of muscle controlled by intelligence drove down the icy mountain track, around high speed turns, and across difficult traverses. Through his years of free skiing at Kitzbühel and elsewhere, he had learned to be light on his skis, to "feel" the snow and adjust his body to it. He had learned to make time in the easier sections of the course and minimize risk where the danger was greatest. He chose his "line" with uncanny precision, and where other racers were side-slipping and flying all over the icy track, Sailer kept himself in check. As he plunged into the finish schuss, the pro-Austrian crowd couldn't contain itself. When Toni's time was announced, hysteria broke loose. He was three and a half seconds faster than the Swiss Raymond Fellay.

Toni Sailer was the first Alpine skier to win three gold medals in the Olympic Games. The huge time margins between him and his adversaries proved his overwhelming superiority. Twenty-year-old Toni Sailer became a national hero overnight and was hailed as the best ski racer in the world.

The following year, Toni Sailer continued to race and win, almost always by large margins. In the 1958 World Ski Championships at Bad Gastein, Austria, he proved that he was still in top form. He won three more world titles. Back home at Kitzbühel, he was modest, well-liked, self-effacing. The town folks treated him more as an ordinary citizen than the great ski racer who had made Kitzbühel famous and all of Austria shine.

His racing career, however, was cut short. Toni Sailer acted in several ski movies and the Fédération Internationale de Ski disqualified him for professionalism. With all of Austria protesting, Sailer retired from competition, studied acting, and eventually made ten films. His autobiography ran through three editions and sold 160,000 copies. Millions of fans saw his films, and when he visited Japan, he was mobbed. A rich man, he returned to Kitzbühel, built a small hotel, became president of the ski club, and in 1972 was appointed head coach of the Austrian ski teams. From then on, whenever an Austrian won a downhill or a slalom race, some of the credit went to Toni Sailer. The Black Angel was still contributing to the glory of Austrian skiing.

☆ ☆ ☆

Toni Sailer had everything in his favor. Highly talented, he grew up in a ski town that had a tradition of ski racing. He raced almost from the time he put on skis. His idols were ski racers, many of whom lived in Kitzbühel. His parents encouraged him. He became part of a ski program that provided expert instruction, good equipment, and organized training for boys his own age. He was encouraged by local, state, and national authorities in a mountainous country where two out of three people skied.

Except for his extraordinary talents, America's Wallace "Bud" Werner had very little in his favor; besides that, he was uncommonly unlucky. Born in 1936—the same year as Sailer—Bud Werner grew up in Steamboat Springs, Colorado. He started skiing when he was four years old and ran his first race at six. He was helped by Gordy Wren who trained the boys in the local ski club. In his book *I Never Look Back,* John Rolfe Burroughs quoted Wren as saying: "Buddy showed more style than the other kids his age, right from the start. He wasn't an easy youngster to teach. He already was developing his own skiing technique, and he was pretty decided about it, too. He never was satisfied with himself—constantly kept trying to improve everything he did in skiing, and everything about his ski equipment. . . . He didn't want any part of second best. But Bud was the direct opposite of being reckless, or careless, or whatever you want to call it. In fact, in planning a race, I've never known another junior skier who studied a course—really mapped it out in his mind and figured out in advance how he was going to run it—as thoroughly as Buddy did. He'd make up his mind how he was going to run a course and then that's precisely the way he ran it. As for his seeming recklessness, it simply was second nature for him to go all out in everything he did—off skis as well as on them. Even as a junior he pulled [out] all the stops. He didn't know any other way to race."

Buddy Werner competed in what fellow racer Tom Corcoran called "a domestic vacuum." In Europe everyone who knew anything about ski racing knew Buddy Werner; few people knew anything about the United States ski team. Only in the later years of Werner's career did the American ski program develop, partly because of the example set by this lone skier who traveled halfway around the world "to beat the Austrians."

Buddy was devoted to whatever he did, and his desire to win was insatiable. He trained himself during the summers by running, doing callisthenics, and climbing telephone poles while working with his father's line crew. Even while he was training he was competing, and that sometimes antagonized the persons he trained with. They were more relaxed than Buddy. Buddy would climb up a slalom hill and show other racers—older or younger—how it was to be done. He was intense and passionate about skiing. He wasn't satisfied to be anything but first, and if he was not first, he often crashed in beautiful fashion. That was his nature, but it was a failing as well.

As a youngster, he was a fine ski jumper. He leaped 285 feet off the giant Howelsen Hill at Steamboat Springs when he was just fifteen years old. The town folk thought he should concentrate on jumping; but the Austrians were downhill and slalom skiers. Buddy wanted to beat them—and on their own ground, on the toughest downhill and slalom *pistes* in the world.

From the beginning, bad luck haunted him. He played trumpet in high school, and one day he got so involved that he fell off the stage and broke an arm. Coach Wren remembers that the following day he showed up as usual for ski practice with his arm in a cast. In 1952, he was probably the finest junior racer in the United States. That year he won the trophy for the best overall performance in downhill, slalom, and jumping in the American Legion Championships. In 1954, he was picked as an alternate on the U.S. team that went to Europe to compete in the World Championships. He was just seventeen years old, and in the downhill he finished in sixth place, behind five Austrians. It was a fantastic performance for a boy his age, but that wasn't good enough for Buddy. The following week at Oslo he won the downhill—the first American male skier to win a major downhill event in Europe.

However, bad luck was never far away. That same year at Åre, Sweden, he sprained an ankle. At the 1956 Cortina Olympics he had a chance to win a medal. He shot down the course, negotiating the difficult sections with ease. But near the bottom he ran into a series of bumps, lost his balance, took a header, lost a ski, bounced back up, and finished. He placed eleventh—the only American in the final standings. After the Olympic Games, he won five straight downhill events and fell in four straight slaloms. The headlines in American and European papers read: "Werner Spills But Wins Ski Race." German sports writers called him "Der Bashful Ski Boy Von Colorado," and the Austrians tellingly nicknamed him *Pechvogel*—the hard-luck kid.

Somehow, between the travel and excitement, Bud managed to finish high school, and for a year or two he flirted with college. He was in and out of the University of Denver, where he was coached by Willy Schaeffler. He also went to the University of Colorado, where he met Bob Beattie, the newly appointed ski coach. Finally,

Bud decided to ski first and to study afterward. Still, the pressures put on him to finish his education and stop being what some considered a ski bum were terrific. According to John Burroughs, Buddy replied: "I know it's not right to delay my education and to lag behind others my age, but I've thought about it, and I know what I'm doing. My one great dream is to be the best skier in the world." In October, 1956, he entered the U.S. Army, and much of his military service was spent on temporary detached duty in Europe.

That year he fell in the Arlberg-Kandahar race at Sestriere, Italy, and tore a ligament. In 1958, at the Bad Gastein World Championships, he finished fourth in the slalom and fifth in the giant slalom. He had a fine chance to be crowned three-event world "combined" champion—a calculation based on points for best placings in downhill, slalom, and giant slalom—but in the downhill he fell a few yards before the finish line. To have that gold medal, another skier would have played it safe, held back just a bit in order to finish, to have silver, if not gold, or even bronze. Not Buddy Werner, though. Buddy Werner said, "There are only two places in a race: first and last. I only want one of them."

His win-or-crash temperament and the bad-luck syndrome continued throughout his life. Training for the Squaw Valley Olympic Games in 1960, he fell and broke a leg. He watched the Winter Olympic Games from the sidelines. He fell again in the World Championships at Chamonix, France, in 1962. And in the 1964 Olympic Games at Innsbruck, after having placed ninth in the first run of the slalom, he fell in the second. Thus, he was never crowned an Olympic or World Championship skier—gold, silver, or bronze —but he was always a threat to the world's best.

His Austrian opponents Anderl Molterer and Karl Schranz said, "The trouble with Buddy is he risks too much. If we were to take all the chances he takes, we'd probably be five seconds faster. But taking all the chances is not the best way to ski in a race."

Buddy couldn't control his temperament. Once on the snow, he went all out and never let up. Fellow teammate Gordie Eaton analyzed it this way: "He couldn't control his emotions, and he would get very intense. In other words, early in the spring when he was rested and had been training, he'd really be relaxed and would do well at the races. As the season went on, he would try harder and harder to do well. He would get tight."

For twelve seasons Buddy Werner traveled from race to race—from the World Championships to the National Championships to the Olympic Games—and he was often alone. He carried his own skis, sharpened his own edges, waxed them himself, trained on his own, and made his own travel and hotel arrangements. If he was listed as a participant in a ski race, the organizers could be sure of a good crowd, good publicity, and some exciting skiing because between the falls and the injuries, Buddy had bursts of brilliance. In 1958 at Wengen, Switzerland, he beat Toni Sailer by an incredible 5.2 seconds in the slalom race, and he went on to take the Lauberhorn combined title—the first American to do so. Teammate Chuck Ferries said, "Either Buddy is over the finish line a full two seconds faster than anyone else, or he is lying out there somewhere on the track."

After he broke his leg at Squaw Valley in 1960, he was virtually finished as a downhiller. With the help of Bob Beattie, the team coach, and some of the younger members of the team, who were fine slalomers, Buddy became one of the team's top slalom contenders.

Buddy Werner ran his last race at Winter Park, Colorado, in March, 1964. At twenty-eight he was still giving all he had in every race, but he had run out of steam and he knew it. Younger racers —Americans Billy Kidd, Chuck Ferries, and Jim Heuga, Austrians Pepi Stiegler and Karl Schranz, the Frenchmen Guy Périllat and Jean-Claude Killy—had made their mark or were moving up. After twelve years on the ski racing circuit, Bud Werner was feeling the pinch of time. The American ski programs were under way and Buddy was destined eventually to take an important role in them. He had married, and it was time to settle down. "This is a good race to quit on," Buddy said, and retired from competition.

But once more he returned to Europe, this time on a pleasure trip. He had been asked by the German Olympic skier Willy Bogner to ski in a film Bogner was making to be called *Holiday on Snow*—a film using the world's top skiers to portray the rhythm and freedom of skiing. The group met at St. Moritz, Switzerland—Bogner, his fiancée Barbi Henneberger from the German Olympic team, Buddy Werner, Fritz Wagnerberger, and ten other of the world's top skiers. It was Sunday, April 12, 1964, when the group caught the funicular to the top of Mount Corviglia, which overlooks St. Moritz. They put on their skis and caught a T-bar lift to the Val Selin, where camera crews prepared platforms for installing equipment. By the time everyone was ready, the sun was up, but the racers, turned actors, were still in the shade of the peaks on wonderful spring snow.

They made a preliminary run and at around ten were back up at the top once again. They were relaxed and joking. This was no race; this was just beautiful fun. Bogner, Henneberger, Werner, and the others began skiing down. Conditions seemed perfect. Suddenly, the slope broke in two, sank a few feet and began to slide. Some of the skiers were able to ski off to the side. Bogner got under a rock to safety. Barbi and Buddy schussed down into the valley in the hopes of outrunning the slide; but at that instant a second avalanche tumbled out of a snow chute, and Barbi and Buddy were gobbled up by the moving mass.

Carried more by the moving snow than by their skis, the other skiers reached the foot of the valley. They counted heads, and someone asked, "Where's Bud? Where's Barbi?" Frantically, they began probing with their skis. A few minutes later rescue crews arrived.

Three hours after the accident the bodies were found. Barbi Henneberger and Bud Werner were dead from shock or suffocation. Said Wagnerberger in an interview shortly after the accident: "It is impossible to express my feelings now. I have known Bud since 1956, and I never saw him laughing so much or having more fun than he did on this trip. He was certainly the finest skier the Americans had. He was also a fantastically boyant young man and a real friend to all of us."

It was early morning in Colorado when the telephone rang. Bud's good friend and coach, Bob Beattie, flew off to Europe to bring his body home. Gordie Eaton was just getting up when the news reached him. "It was like nine-thirty in the morning. It was one of those things that you hear and, you know, you just refuse to believe it. It just does not mean anything to you. It can't happen. And then you sit down and think about it for a little while and you just start to cry because at that point . . . that was the first person that had ever died that I knew; I couldn't accept it. It was a person who was just a good human being. Ski racing did not have anything to do with it. He was just a good human being."

Funeral services were held in Steamboat Springs attended by Werner's family and thousands of his friends. The American pioneer was gone from the scene he had helped to create. Later on, so that his example would not be forgotten, Bud Werner ski leagues for promising junior racers were set up in many mountain areas all over the United States, and the Bud Werner Memorial Race became a part of the international racing calendar. These institutions are a living testimony to this human being who did so much in his short life to popularize ski racing in the United States.

☆ ☆ ☆

In the middle of the summer of 1966, the Alpine World Championships were held for the first time at the relatively isolated resort of Portillo in Chile. In the Southern Hemisphere, it was, of course, winter, but Portillo was so far away from any big ski-oriented city that the 1966 events became known as the championships nobody saw. In any event, the races were covered by television, the wire services, and a few hearty ski journalists from the Alpine lands. So the news poured out of Chile while most of the skiing public were on summer vacation. The French learned that a skier from Val d'Isère, Jean-Claude Killy, had won a gold medal in the downhill as well as the overall three-event combined title. The French team as a whole had been awarded sixteen out of twenty-four possible medals. Never before had any ski team won so many medals, either in the World Championships or in the Olympic Games.

After the team had returned to France, a motor parade was held in the city of Grenoble, where the Olympic Games were scheduled for 1968. Fifty thousand people lined the streets, and the ingrained chauvinism of the French burst forth. This was the greatest sports victory of any French team since the country was founded! France was the greatest skiing country in the world! And, besides, the country had a new hero known by teen-agers and octogenarians alike: Jean-Claude Killy—tall, blond, square-jawed, modest—who was destined to outdo the ski exploits of the best that Austria, Switzerland, or any other country had ever produced!

Not everybody shared the enthusiasm of the French over their team and their hero. Some American, Austrian, and Swiss racers and some journalists and technicians who made up the giant caravan of cars and trucks that followed the ski circuit in the mountains from December to April were not convinced that Jean-Claude Killy was really the greatest thing going. An Austrian journalist is quoted in Michel Clare's biography entitled *Jean-Claude Killy* as having written the following about Killy's Portillo triumphs: "Killy's downhill victory doesn't mean a thing because the downhill *piste* was not at all a true test of technique. It will be curious to see how well the French do on the real downhill *pistes* at Wengen and Kitzbühel."

When asked what he thought of this statement, Jean-Claude Killy refused to answer. Within himself he knew he had been getting stronger, not only in the slalom and giant slalom, but also in the downhill events, which traditionally were Austria's forte.

After a three-week rest, Killy began to train meticulously for the 1967 winter season. Not only were there the "classic" races at Wengen, Kitzbühel, Megève, and a long series of events in the United States, but for the first time a World Alpine Ski Cup was at stake. To be crowned World Cup champion, a skier had to win or place well in the slalom, downhill, and giant slalom events throughout the season. Killy had decided that he wanted that cup and the satisfactions that came with being the best in the world. But even more than that, he wanted to prove that his Portillo win was no stroke of good luck.

Success was no stranger to Jean-Claude Killy. He was brought up in Val d'Isère, France, by a father who dreamed that his son would be a world ski champion. But what distinguished Robert Killy from other parents was that he provided the motivation for his son and then let the environment of the budding Val d'Isère ski area do the rest. When Jean-Claude made his first contact with the snow, he went wild. Robert Killy nicknamed his son Toutoune— the name suggested a young wolf—and he gave the boy a fine pair of skis and the freedom to use them.

When he was eight years old, Jean-Claude won a trophy for ski jumping; at nine he won a gold *Chamois* medal, beating the pace setter's time by a full second. Winning a gold *Chamois* at that age in France is like winning the NASTAR championships in the United States. (NASTAR races, open to recreational skiers of all ages, are held in many U.S. ski resorts. Through a process of elimination, the winners of races eventually compete on a national level.) When Jean-Claude was ten years old, he won a regional race, and his downhill time outdistanced that of his nearest rival by nine seconds. His picture was in the newspapers—a prediction of things to come.

But before total victory, misfortune and discouragement had to be conquered. When he was fourteen, in his first international race at Cortina, Italy, he broke his left leg and lost a season's racing. At sixteen, he became a member of the French Talent Squad, a selected group of young racers whom the coaches feel have the potential to become members of the national team. The following year he won all the gold medals at the French Junior Championships. By the end of 1961, he was selected for the French ski team, but he broke his leg once again and did not race in 1962.

In 1963, after a six-month stint in the army in Algeria, where he caught jaundice, Killy racked up an impressive series of second places in international competitions, which made him a sure choice for the 1964 Olympic team. At Innsbruck, however, he had bad luck. He placed fifth in the giant slalom, but in the slalom he ripped the binding clear off his ski and was disqualified. For the moment, medals were not for him.

In 1965, though, he was back on the podiums. After a second place in the Lauberhorn slalom, he won the Hahnenkamm combined title at Kitzbühel and the combined at Megève. On the American circuit, he placed first in the Bud Werner Memorial Race, but his first visit to the States brought him other recompenses. From the American racers Jim Heuga and Billy Kidd, Killy learned some important things about the mental attitude that goes into ski racing. "They are so relaxed," he said, "and have fun all the time in competition, and I learned to imitate them." And later he said: "One should never forget that ski racing is a game. One has to give oneself to it with passion without giving it an excessive importance."

The following year, 1966, was a good one, with wins in all the classic slalom races in Europe and in many American races as well. But up until his downhill breakthrough at Portillo, Toutoune had never won a major downhill event.

In preparing for the 1967 season, Jean-Claude spent long hours choosing his equipment. Together with former teammate Michel Arpin, he tested skis, boots, poles, even clothing. Both racers had recognized the essential change that had taken place in ski racing since the time of Toni Sailer. What counted in the 1960's was tenths, even hundredths, of seconds; and these differences between the very good and the champion racers, between gold and silver, could often be found in the human judgment and skill that went into the manufacture and preparation of equipment. During training sessions, Arpin was a familiar figure on the sides of the *piste,* stopwatch in hand, timing his friend through key sections of each racecourse. From 1966 until Killy retired in 1968, Arpin was Killy's personal coach. He selected Killy's skis, mounted Killy's bindings, sharpened his edges, and waxed his skis before races. Later on, Killy said, "Without Michel Arpin I never would have won three gold medals in the Olympic Games." Arpin, who had never won a major international race while on the French team, was to have his moments of glory as Killy's personal manager. "Through me," Killy wrote, "he was world champion and triple Olympic champion. I owe him these titles."

By the time the 1967 season opened, Jean-Claude Killy was not only in top form physically, but he also had confidence in his equipment and in his ability to prove to the world that he was the best. At Adelboden, Switzerland, he won the season's first giant slalom, giving him twenty-five points in the World Cup standings. Then the troupe went on to Wengen.

But Killy was feeling the pressure. At Wengen, the Lauberhorn downhill was two and a half miles long, full of high-speed turns and huge bumps interrupted by relatively flat forest trails where you had to maintain maximum speed. The Lauberhorn racecourse and the Hahnenkamm Streif are probably the most difficult and exhausting downhill courses in the world, and his competitors—Austrians Schranz and Nenning, the Swiss Jos Minsch, the American Billy Kidd, and the German Franz Volger, as well as his own teammates Léo Lacroix and Guy Périllat—were not exactly pushovers. The night before the race, he confided in the French journalist Michel Clare: "I'm playing double or nothing," he said, indicating that he would go all out in the race. "If I win, I'll be calm for the rest of the season because this downhill is not exactly to my liking." Killy was particularly worried about his ability to slide well on the flats. At the start he summoned up all his courage, planted his poles, and leaped out of the starting gate. He ran the Lauberhorn perfectly and won. The following day, calm and collected, Toutoune took the slalom with ease, giving him the combined title with the optimum point score of zero. Including the twenty-five giant slalom points from Adelboden, in one week's time he had amassed seventy-five World Cup points.

The following weekend, true to his prediction, he won the Hahnenkamm downhill on the Strief, the slalom, and the combined. The weekend after that he added the Megève downhill to his record and placed second in the slalom. He went on to the Kandahar at Sestriere, Italy, and won the downhill and combined. Journalists no longer were concerned as to who was going to win each race. That was a foregone conclusion. Killy so dominated the competition that the question became: "Who will place second and third?"

The "ski-circus," as it was called, left Europe for the United States, where Killy's name had become popular through articles in large circulation magazines. Killy had become an international star; still he had to prove that the journalists were not wrong. In the nine United States races, Jean-Claude won eight. The Austrians said: "The French as a whole are not better than we are. It is only Killy who has dominated all of us!" At the United States National Championships, to which Killy was invited, Jean-Claude won the three major titles and the combined as well. Before the season's end, he had wrapped up skiing's first World Cup, having attained the maximum number of points in each specialty. Killy had won skiing's grand slam.

Clearly, this was the most outstanding season any ski racer had ever had. Not only did Toutoune win ski races, but he also captured the imagination of the public—in Europe, in the United States, and wherever people skied. With his long blond hair, his casual manner, and his frankness, which came across even over television, Toutoune became an idol.

The following year he increased his fame by winning three gold medals in the Olympic Games at Grenoble and his second World Cup. By then, Jean-Claude Killy had nothing more to win or to prove through further competition. He had equalled Toni Sailer's three-medal victory. At twenty-four, the man who was the best in the world retired from competition.

But Killy was never destined to retire to some Alpine ski area as a director of operations. He kept his name in the public's mind through endorsements of products and personal appearances. He chalked up another win: he was the first ski racer to become a millionaire. He was rich and famous. He owned a mansion on Lake Geneva in Switzerland and an apartment in Paris; he had property at Val d'Isère, and he directed a ski area in the United States, where he spent six months of the year. Still, Killy wasn't satisfied. He missed the competition of racing, preparing his body, mind, and equipment for the race. He talked to Bob Beattie, the former American coach who had set up a professional ski racers' association. In 1972–73 Killy joined the pros and raced again—not so much for the money, but rather for the happiness and satisfaction that racing had always given him. Even after a four-year layoff and in new kinds of races like head-to-head parallel slaloms and giant slaloms with built-in jumps involving new techniques, Killy came back to beat the pros just as he had the amateurs. Once again he was the number one skier in the world, and this time in one season he added close to $100,000 to his fortune.

In Europe or America, where ski racing was still dominated by the so-called amateurs and their federations, the debate went on:

Who had been the greatest ski racer of all time—Austria's Toni Sailer or France's Jean-Claude Killy? Both had dominated Olympic Games, both were world champions, both had won all the great ski races at least once, and both were still involved in ski racing. To a certain extent, the answer to the question depended on where you lived and when you were born. The older generation preferred Sailer, the younger generation the skier from Val d'Isère who was groomed to be a winner.

☆ ☆ ☆

No other skier in the world had as long a career crowned with so many victories as the Austrian Karl Schranz. After seventeen years in active international competition, there wasn't a single great race that Schranz had not won at least once, and several of them he won many times. If Bud Werner's career was haunted by bad luck and Jean-Claude Killy's highlighted by outstanding success, Karl Schranz's was filled with controversy.

It all began in 1954. Karl Schranz was sixteen years old and he had just won the Junior World Slalom Championship. He was hailed, and rightly so, as a child prodigy and future great. In 1957, he won his first Kandahar, and the following year he was almost certain to win a medal at the World Championships. A bad case of the grippe prevented his being selected for the team, but he recovered sufficiently to make two runs, which opened up the two courses. In both runs Schranz bettered the times of teammate Toni Sailer, who eventually swept all the medals. An exploit like this was not ignored by the public or the press.

Four years later, Schranz was to prove that his Bad Gastein performance was no fluke. At the Chamonix World Championships, Schranz won the downhill and combined medals; and at the 1966 and 1970 World Ski Championships he picked up two more medals. Each season he added victory to victory. He won the famed Kandahar downhill race eight times and the combined five times, the Lauberhorn downhill four times and the combined twice, the Hahnenkamm downhill three times and the combined twice. In 1969 and 1970 he won the World Cup and was crowned the world's greatest skier. But by fate or accident the Olympic gold medal always eluded him. The Olympic Games seemed to bring out his weaknesses. Squaw Valley (1960) produced poor performances and an avowal to quit racing. Innsbruck (1964) gave him a silver medal in giant slalom, but, in the magazine *Profil* a disappointed Schranz was quoted as saying, "Only the gold medal would have meant a success for me." When at Grenoble (1968) Schranz was disqualified after he believed he had won the slalom, his love for ski racing turned to hate and disgust. And his prohibition at the last moment from competing at the 1972 Sapporo, Japan, games was one of the greatest injustices ever committed by the International Olympic Committee.

Economic conditions were very bad in Austria in November, 1938, when Karl Schranz was born at St. Anton. Karl's father, who was badly paid and often ill, worked on the railroad as a maintenance worker. His mother kept up the family farm and raised five children. They were poor, so poor that to this day Karl Schranz does not like to talk about those years.

Karl started skiing when he was able to walk. His father repaired a pair of skis that a tourist had left behind, and when the boy was four years old, he won his first race. Subsequently, when he did not win he was in a state of gloom. Karl Schranz said, "If you were born in St. Anton and you were poor, there was nothing else for you to do but to try to become a ski racer."

When he was eight years old, the farm burned down and his family became even poorer. Still, nothing prevented Karl from running in the fields to tune his muscles or skiing into the night and coming home exhausted. Said former coach Professor Hopplicher in 1971, "It is exactly this terrible poverty which motivated Schranz and continues to motivate him . . ."

Toni Sailer, Bud Werner, Billy Kidd, Jean-Claude-Killy, Jean Saubert, the Goitschel sisters, Nancy Greene, and the other great ski racers also had that essential drive to win; but in none of them was it emphasized so profoundly as in Karl Schranz. It dominated him and became an obsession: "It is only when I am on the highest step of the podium that I feel at ease," Schranz said. "I race to win, and no other place but first gives me real joy." To be first was essential to his pride and was his reason for living.

It was exactly this monomania that alienated Schranz from his team members. They could respect his courage, his will, and his determination; but it was hard, if not impossible, to get close to Schranz the man. That was the last thing "Karli" wanted. Karl's attitude was: "If I say that I must win at any price, and if another says the same thing, it is impossible that that person can be my friend, because I must win. If I haven't got that will power, it's not worth the trouble to start a race." Racing for Schranz became a question of one will against another. The truth lay in the flying seconds of the timekeepers' clocks. "I always race against other people, other racers, rather than the terrain," he said.

Karl Schranz was relatively short and lithe and had a tremendous pair of thigh muscles. When he was on a downhill course, you could see that he was relaxed. He knew exactly where to start a high-speed turn in order to take the fastest "line" lower down. When he schussed into the finish area, he would turn around and look, first up the course, remembering every turn, bump, and patch of ice, and then his steely eyes would gaze at the board to catch his time. If he won, he would smile and receive the ovations of the crowd and the solicitations of friends and journalists; but if he was second or third, which meant that he had lost, he was often inaccessible.

To support that terrible obsession to be the best, Schranz trained and raced at least nine months a year. He trained even between the regularly organized training periods of the Austrian team, when he was supposed to rest. He could be seen at St. Anton running through the fields with lead weights on his back. He was a fanatic for training. He loved the pain at the time and the glory of the wins later on. Training, skiing, racing, standing on podiums was his life. He never smoked or drank; and from July to April he rarely went out with women. For ski racing, he controlled all his pleasures.

When he was seventeen years old, he went to see magnate Franz Kneissl. Kneissl, recognizing Schranz's talents and devotion to ski racing, gave him a job as a sawmill apprentice. Throughout his long career, Schranz skied on Kneissl skis and worked closely with the company's engineers and technicians to perfect material and develop new ways of going faster. In the off-track race to cut hundredths of seconds from his time, he wore aerodynamic clothing, special test skis, and a pointed helmet. He was one of the first racers to test equipment in wind tunnels. Since with Schranz victory was always possible, several technicians—from ski designers to wax specialists—were permanently assigned to him. Their job was to make certain that not only was his equipment the best available, but also that on the *pistes* Schranz was taking the fastest possible "line" down the mountain.

Without a doubt one of Schranz's great gifts was an incredible ability, over a period of seventeen years, to adapt his style to changes in technique and material. As the ski journalist Serge Lang remarked: "He won his first races at the average speed of forty-three miles an hour, and thirteen years later he was still winning races which had an average speed of sixty-five miles per hour." This talent was largely responsible for keeping him on or near the top for so many years.

Schranz's fame helped "patron" Kneissl sell skis. Paid well for this, Schranz was able to build a pension-hotel at St. Anton and move his mother into a comfort she had rarely known. It was rumored that as an "amateur" Schranz made close to $100,000 per year from the manufacturers who supplied him with equipment. Half of that figure is probably closer to the truth. Undoubtedly, some of this money went into the Austrian team coffers, but a lot of it came back home. He drove around the Alps in a sparkling Porsche or a Jaguar, and it was no rumor that, financially speaking, the Arlberg Monk, as he was called, was no longer hurting.

For seventeen years, Schranz raced on the Austrian National Ski Team. He won, was cheered by millions all over the world, was greeted by national and world political leaders, and was feted by officials. But unlike Toni Sailer or France's Jean Claude Killy, Karl Schranz was never popular with his teammates nor was he able to capture the love and imagination of the public. He commanded respect, even awe because of his indomitable will to win and be the best. He was often the center of bitter controversies between teammates, team leaders, federation officials, and ski equipment manufacturers. He was called everything from a prima donna to a snob, but Schranz weathered it all and kept on racing—the only thing he knew.

During the ups and downs of his long career, one trophy—the Olympic gold medal—had always eluded him. He came closest at Grenoble in 1968. The fog at the Chamrousse ski area was thick when Schranz, trailing Killy by a few hundredths of a second after the first run in the slalom, began his second attempt. The clocks ticked off seconds, and Schranz did not come out of the fog. The speaker announced that the Austrian star claimed he had been hindered during his run by the dark shadow of a spectator on the foggy course and that the jury had decided to give him another chance, pending their official meeting after the race. Schranz climbed back up the course and this time bettered Killy's two-run overall time. With the Olympic gold medal practically hanging around his neck, Schranz went berserk. He waved at the crowds, kissed his trainers, and threw his arms up giving the photographers and all concerned a great show. An Austrian—Karl Schranz— had prevented Jean-Claude Killy from equaling Toni Sailer's triple victory in 1956. Austria was still the greatest skiing power in the world, and Schranz, the poor boy from the Arlberg, had proved it.

But it wasn't to be. The jury ruled that on his first try in the second run, Schranz was so far away from "the shadow," which theoretically crossed the track in front of him, that it would not have caused him to miss two gates. Schranz was disqualified. Killy took top place on the podium and said, "I would have been content with a silver medal." *Ski Magazine* in Spring, 1968, reported Schranz's reply at a press conference: "If Killy were sportsmanlike, he would refuse the gold medal to which I have the right."

The bitter Franco-Austrian controversy continued for many months. Killy retired from "amateur" competition and rapidly became a millionaire. Karl Schranz, down but not out, went on racing. In 1969 and 1970, when he won the World Cup, he announced that he would terminate his career after the 1972 Olympic Games in Sapporo, Japan. He still wanted that gold medal.

"The Arlberg Monk" trained harder than ever. He won the first major downhill of the season at Val d'Isère, beating a host of great French, Swiss, and American downhillers like Duvillard, Russi, and Mike Lafferty. Then, on the Streif *piste* at Kitzbühel, Schranz racked up two consecutive downhill victories. "Super Schranz is in super form for Sapporo," cried the Austrian press joyfully as the team left for Japan. Meanwhile, the threat of disqualification by the International Olympic Committee for violating the Olympic amateur rules hung over the heads of many ski racers. Schranz was number one on the list.

Training began on the far-away snows of Sapporo, while the seventy-second session of the International Olympic Committee convened to discuss, among other business, the disqualification question. Schranz didn't help his cause very much when, in an Associated Press report, he stated: "If Mr. Brundage [then the president of the IOC] had been poor like I and several other athletes were, I wonder if his attitude would be different." Schranz went on to criticize the domination of the IOC by wealthy aristocrats and the conflict of Olympic ideals with everyday realities.

Then the ax fell. The IOC singled out Schranz and declared that he had used his fame to publicize ski equipment. In their opinion, he was no longer an amateur. He was the only ski racer banned from the eleventh winter games, from any chance of ever winning an Olympic medal. Said Schranz in an AP report: "This time I believed I really had a chance to win. This decision has hurt me even more than the decision at Grenoble where I found myself in the deepest gloom. It is a true injustice; I am not either more or less an amateur than the others, all the others. Why have they chosen me as an example, me who loves skiing so much?"

Banishment was a strange way for a great ski racer to terminate a long career. The amateur-professional question, long a thorn in the side of the international organizations that rule all sports, was bound to remain a preoccupation for years to come. The establishment of a professional ski circuit in the United States, which was attracting some of the world's best skiers who preferred honesty to hypocrisy, would certainly have an effect on amateur racing. Many top amateurs were threatening to turn pro. If they did, this could destroy the prestige of amateur racing. Karl

Schranz was one of the victims of a bureaucracy that could not make up its mind and come to grips with the real problems of modern skiers. For the best, ski racing had become a way of life, a profession like any other, which did not cease at age twenty-one or two. Ski racers, like Karl Schranz, proved through devotion, will, and intelligence that ski racing was more than just a short period in a man's life. For a very few, it was life itself.

☆ ☆ ☆

There was something special about Nancy Greene, something that distinguished her from all the other racers during the 1960's. Everyone felt it—the journalists, trainers, racers, technicians—the whole caravan of people who followed the circuit from country to country and continent to continent in planes, buses, and cars for six months of the year. For a long time the Canadian's career, which lasted ten years, was overshadowed by that of Jean-Claude Killy. Besides that, up until 1967, Nancy was often beaten by Marielle Goitschel, the French great, or Christl Haas, the Austrian Olympic downhill champion. But Nancy Greene was a fighter, and she kept plugging away, season after season, injury after injury, like Schranz trying to win an Olympic gold or like Buddy Werner trying to win a title and help ski racing catch on in the United States. She was wonderfully naïve and correct, used words like "heck," "neat," "real," and "darn"—a kind of wide-eyed hillbilly from the Canadian West, endowed with tremendous talent and dogged determination.

Like all great ski racers, Nancy Greene had a terrible will to win and a classic sense of fair play and sportsmanship, which came through so clearly, particularly in the later years of her career. More than that, I think that, unlike many other great ski racers, she grew into the role of champion; that is, her technical skills improved in conjunction with her developing maturity as a woman. When she became a champion, she had already grown into a richer, broader human being. By then she was not only the greatest ski racer that Canada had ever produced, but also the best woman racer in the world. At the end of the 1968 season, ski racing had nothing more to teach her about herself, and she retired.

It took her almost ten years to reach those heights. She was born in Rossland, British Columbia, in 1944. Up until she was fourteen years old, Nancy Greene was just a recreational skier on the town's Red Mountain. Ski racing just didn't interest her because she liked free skiing and because her older sister Liz was on the Canadian national team, which overwhelmed Nancy. But in 1958 the Canadian National Junior Championships were held in Rossland, and several of the racers were out of action because of injury and sickness. The night before the championships the local coach telephoned Nancy and asked if she would be willing to race, to fill out the team. Nancy agreed. The following day she entered the slalom and finished third. Sister Liz was first. Then they ran the downhill. Nancy was second, Liz first. Nancy was carried away by the excitement of ski racing, and the rivalry to beat her sister bloomed.

Two years later, both Liz and Nancy were selected for the Canadian Olympic team, which was led by Anne Heggtveit. Nancy was just sixteen and was awed by the pagentry of the Squaw Valley games and the skills of competitors like the German downhiller Heidi Biebl and the American Penny Pitou. And for a sixteen-year-old, Nancy didn't do badly: twenty-sixth in the giant slalom, thirty-first in the slalom, and the third best Canadian in the downhill. But for her and the rest of the Canadian team, the highlight of the games was when teammate Heggtveit won the slalom. When Anne stepped up onto the podium to receive her medal, with the Canadian national anthem playing in the background, Nancy burst into tears and resolved that one day she would win an Olympic medal. It was to take her eight more years and a lot of heartbreaks and inner probing before she would realize her dream.

In 1961 neighbors and friends from Rossland contributed the money necessary to send Nancy Greene and another racer, Verne Anderson (the following year he became Canadian coach), to race in Europe. Nancy learned a lot on the ski circuit, but she won no races. Instead, she returned to race in the United States National Championships at Sun Valley and broke her leg. Nancy went back to Rossland and finished high school. During her recuperation period, she began training by lifting weights. She kept up these exercises throughout her career until for her 125 pounds, she was the strongest member on the Canadian team, including the men.

During the next four years she won occasional races—mostly "B" events on the European or American circuits. But it was not until 1965 that an important change took place. As the season wore on, she kept improving. That year the United States National Championships were held at Crystal Mountain, Washington, and many French and Austrian racers were invited. Their participation gave the championships an international flavor and permitted North American racers, who had not been able to participate in the European classics, not only a chance to improve their seed standing on the FIS lists, but also an opportunity to see the world's best in action. Canada's Nancy Greene won the slalom and giant slalom titles. In the slalom she outdistanced her arch rival Marielle Goitschel, the 1964 Olympic champion, by a full second. "From that moment on," she said in a recent interview, "I no longer worried about if I could win; it was just a question of whether I was going to." The psychological difference between "if" and "whether" is an essential one to a ski racer of world-class calibre.

Nancy Greene was the American and Canadian woman's champion, but world and Olympic titles continued to elude her. In the 1962 and 1966 World Championships, and in the 1960 and 1964 Olympic Games, she either failed miserably or turned in mediocre performances. In Chamonix in 1962 she finished fifth in the downhill; in the 1964 Innsbruck Olympics, where she felt she had a good chance to win a medal, she waxed her skis badly and finished in seventh place, almost four seconds behind Austrian winner Christl Haas. At that point everyone, including Nancy's parents, expected her to give up ski racing; but Nancy was still learning and, more than anything else, she wanted to have one more crack at the world and Olympic titles.

In 1966 she had a good year on the European circuit and won several races, beating both Goitschel sisters in the slalom at Bad Gastein. But at the August World Championships at Portillo,

Chile, she crashed fifty yards from the finish and tore the ligaments in her elbow. Add to that defeat a seventh place in the slalom and a fourth in the giant slalom, and Portillo was just plain bad news for Nancy.

Despite her Portillo failures, Nancy Greene was striving not just to win an occasional race but to win regularly. She describes her feelings about this in her autobiography, which was published late in 1968: "Any skier with good technique, no matter how young she is, can win a race at one time or another; but the test is to win consistently, against all competition, where there is pressure on you to win." When the great Austrian ski racer Annemarie Proell was asked who among all the ski racers in the world she admired most of all, the three-time winner of the World Cup replied, "Nancy Greene—she was consistent."

If you were to ask Canadian ski fans what Nancy Greene's greatest race was they would undoubtedly say the final race of the 1967 season—the first year the World Alpine Ski Cup was offered. Before the race, held at Jackson Hole, Wyoming, and called the Wild West Classic, two French racers—Marielle Goitschel and Anne Famose—had 169 and 158 World Cup points respectively, and Canada's Nancy Greene was in third position with 151. Theoretically, Nancy had a chance to win the World Cup, but to do so, she had to win the two giant slalom races and the slalom, either to chalk up points or to prevent the French stars from gaining additional points. Nancy's chances were very slim, but she was strong in the giant slalom, and she went all out in those races held on Friday and Saturday. She won both of them; but to win the cup, she needed the slalom victory as well. In other words, three wins in three days against the world's best ski racers was what was required.

The pressure on Nancy Greene was tremendous. She did not sleep very much on Saturday night. After the first run of Sunday's slalom she was in second place behind French slalom specialist Florence Steurer. Marielle Goitschel was in third place just 9/100ths of a second off the leader's time.

With the pressure building up by the minute, the three slalom leaders waited impatiently for the start of the race. Nancy, with a low start number, got ready to get into the starting gate. "Good luck," said Marielle. "May the best one win." Nancy Greene looked up and felt like replying that indeed *she* would win. Meanwhile, the speaker on the public address system built up tension among the spectators and racers alike by emphasizing time and again how important this final race was for Nancy. By winning she would win skiing's first World Cup and with it world recognition as the greatest woman ski racer in the world. "I knew that I had to win standing in the start gate at the second run of the slalom. But all of a sudden it was as if I was someone else, and I just started to laugh inside and there was just this tremendous euphoric feeling, and Marielle said: 'Good luck' and I was laughing almost all the way down the course because I thought that if this was the most important thing in my life, then this was going to be a pretty dumb life. I think that that was the moment, as far as being able to control my nerves and everything else, that was the most important moment in my racing career. Everything went into perspective." Nancy Greene won the slalom, the 1967 World Cup, and pandemonium broke loose.

Nancy Greene continued racing and winning consistently throughout the 1968 season, and she went on to win her second World Cup. She won the downhill, the slalom, and the combined at the Chamonix Kandahar, the three events at Sun Valley and at Aspen, the giant slalom at Rossland, and so on. But in the downhill at the Grenoble, France, Olympics, once again she waxed her skis badly and skied a bad race besides. She finished in tenth place, almost three seconds back. She had a good cry and a couple of days later took a silver medal in the slalom. That gave her confidence—the boost she needed for the giant slalom. "I hadn't lost a giant slalom race in a year and a half. Everything was perfect. I remembered the course, I had perfect skis and equipment. I've seen the film of the race since then and I cannot see any place where I would have changed and skied it differently. I didn't make any mistakes. I used all my strong points to my advantage. I worked terribly hard in the race. At the finish, my legs were so tired I could hardly stand up. I looked up at the scoreboard and looked at my time and I was the highest on the board and I was so relieved, and it wasn't happiness, but I knew it was the best I could possibly have done."

Nancy Greene, with an advance of almost three seconds over her nearest rival, was clearly head and shoulders above the competition.

2
THE MEANING OF WORLD CUP SKI RACING

The racers come from all over the world, from Japan, New Zealand, and Australia, from Canada and the United States, from Great Britain and the Alpine countries, where skiing is a major sport, from South America, Russia, Poland, Andorra, and San Marino. They all have different talents and strengths, different equipment, educations, professions, upbringing, and religions. But they all have one idea: participate in and do well on the World Cup circuit.

Only a few of them can honestly hope to win, but many of the others believe that they can work themselves up through the ranks and improve their technique and seeding to the point that victory becomes possible. Brilliant sixteen-year-old girls challenge twenty-five-year-old veterans in the old battle of youth versus age in an individual sport where each race can yield but one winner.

The participants may include a farmer's boy from Kufstein, a mechanic's daughter from Flums, an engineer's son from Vermont—all good enough to represent their countries in international competitions often held thousands of miles from their homes. They travel the ski circuit for four months over three continents—two hundred of the world's best ski racers—shuttling from hotel to hotel, from pensions and boarding houses to condominiums, ranches, chalets—carrying hundred-pound ski bags, living in crowded rooms out of suitcases, eating different kinds of foods, and trying to communicate in ten different languages. It is an exhausting, frustrating, exciting challenge to put mind, talent, and equipment together in order to go a few seconds faster on race day.

Some of the racers from the poorer ski associations are roughing it—traveling by the cheapest means possible to the border of the country where the next race will be held because from that point their expenses will be paid by the race organizers. They have little pocket money and have to chase after the suppliers of equipment for ski boots, poles, clothing; and then they have to convince the manufacturers' representatives that they, too—the underdogs—have a chance to do well and deserve attention.

They point to some of the great non-Alpine country champions —Stein Erickson, Chick Igaya, Malcolm Milne, Nancy Greene— and they ask: Why not us? In many cases, these smaller association racers—men and women from Japan, Australia, Spain, the Nordic countries, and Chile—have no coach, trainer, or entourage of any sort. They either attach themselves to one of the big teams or take care, as best they can, of administrative details. They attend the daily race meetings where start orders, race times, seedings, training sessions, and other matters of vital importance are discussed and decided. While on the mountain they have little encouragement, and there is no one around to correct their faults. They have to work themselves up the ladder the hard way, and in many cases they return to their countries and enter another profession. For them, though, it is a fling, a chance, a period in life when they can pit themselves against the Alpine country greats—and see the very special world of ski racing at the same time.

The richer ski associations—from Austria, France, Italy, Switzerland, and sometimes the United States (depending on fund-raising successes and the whims of the administrators)—train and travel in style. At one race during the 1973 season, the Italian men's team was ferried five miles from the Swiss resort of Wengen to Grindelwald by rented helicopter in order to avoid a bothersome two-hour train ride around the mountain to the downhill start. The Alpine land heroes and heroines are treated with silk gloves

—the best hotels, food, equipment, and, more important, the personnel to keep the equipment and them in top shape—trainers, coaches, and ski technicians, working with two-way radios and portable video machines, which make possible reruns of key sections of a course during training sessions, giving all the attention possible to help the racer do his thing—race, sleep, concentrate, and leave the calculating and menial jobs to trained specialists who are being paid by manufacturers or ski associations to do just that.

Why? Why all the special care and kid-gloving? When Alpine country ski racers were closer to being amateurs—in the 1930's and 1940's—they had one or two pairs of skis, one pair of boots, and they traveled short distances to races that usually took place during their winter vacations. There were two or three important races a year, and that was it. Since those days, ski racing has moved into the big time, which means into the manufacturers' fight for international ski markets, for ski equipment is being sold all over the world—Head or Rossignol skis in Japan, Kazamas in the United States, Kneissls in Australia, and Lange boots in Chile. The big time also means wide-spread publicity for Alpine resorts where races are held. Television beams ski race coverage to Africa and South America. And resorts like Jackson Hole, Chamonix, St. Anton, and Sapporo hope that tourists will eventually visit and ski the great runs they offer. Numbers of races have increased and are held all over the world. The international calendar during the 1972-73 season listed fourteen World Cup race meetings for men and fourteen for women in ten countries, with twenty-four races for men and twenty-four for women. Besides that, there are European Cup races in Europe and Can-Am races in Canada and the United States, whose purpose is to provide a minor league training ground for younger racers and veterans who want to sharpen their techniques. And after the four-month top-season grind is over, there are important summer events in Southern Hemisphere countries like Chile, Australia, and New Zealand, as well as on the glaciers of Austria, France, and Switzerland. These low-key races are meant to keep the men and women in condition and in a competitive frame of mind.

By the 1970's World Cup ski racing was no longer a two-week

or even a two-month affair; it had become a yearly occupation, and this fact had serious ramifications on racers all over the world. It meant that a racer, if he wanted to compete in the big time, had to train at least six months of the year and race for four. That meant that ski racing could in no sense of the word be considered a pastime or amateur sport; it was a profession. It meant that during those ten months of the year a racer had to be supported by the ski associations, ski equipment manufacturers, his family, or private contributors. For the Europeans this was never very much of a problem. Ski racing on the continent had always been regarded as a respectable profession for which a racer was supported. But in North America, where finishing high school and attending college was an accepted part of our way of life, ski racing was not regarded in the same way. Being a ski racer most of the year meant a break with tradition.

In the late 1960's and early 1970's some American and Canadian racers simply decided that ski racing was more important than going to college. Others attended college (where they undoubtedly had a scholarship) for one or two quarters a year and took six to eight years to get a diploma. What it came down to was that if you wanted to ski-race and hoped to compete on equal ground against the Alpine country talents, you had to put off your education at least for a time.

Before the World Cup circuit existed, races were held in the Alpine lands and in North America (with scanty European participation), and every two years there was either a World Championship meeting organized by the FIS or a Winter Olympic Games. On the basis of one race, ski racers were crowned. If you were in top form on that particular day, you won your race and medal. If you were off form, you had to wait another two years or retire from competition an uncrowned non-hero. But officials and racers recognized the inequalities involved in a one-race-or-nothing philosophy. Ski racing was an individual sport with strong psychological ups and downs. The best racer did not always win an Olympic gold medal. Something else was needed, and the answer was the World Cup, to be awarded to the best overall skiers in the world, based on the season's performance.

Racers liked the idea because it gave meaning to a hard season's work, and ski equipment suppliers liked the idea because it gave them annual champions and the chance to publicize them—overtly or covertly. To a manufacturer—who supplied hundreds of free pairs of skis per year to the big ski associations and to individual racers and who paid money into the association "pools" for the right to advertise that his equipment was being used by the national team—a World Cup win meant the difference between successful advertising campaigns involving the possible sale of fifty thousand pairs of skis or no campaign at all. The same was true for manufacturers of boots, bindings, poles, and clothing equipment. The companies were in World Cup competition not particularly for the glory but rather for the markets to be gained and the money to be made.

The caravans got larger. Television got in on the act. Big money was at stake. It was called the White Circus—a descendant of the traveling groups of gypsies, minstrels, clowns, and acrobats who used to wander from land to land with their acts, going south in winter, north in summer. Only the ski circus was different. The skiers were there not so much to entertain as to win or work themselves up the ladder to a point where they could shoot for the top. World Cup ski racing was a deadly serious business, particularly for the Europeans who had dominated Alpine racing for fifty years and who were not yet ready to accept the professional ski racing circuit created by Bob Beattie, the former coach of the United States ski teams.

For the racers, who had become the instruments of the big interests, winning the World Cup was more important than winning an Olympic or World Championship medal. The World Cup demanded consistent high placings in competitions spread over a four-month period. There weren't many world class skiers who could do well in three events; but for those who could, their futures were assured. Back in the late 1950's Toni Sailer was big time, and then Jean-Claude Killy made his million; Karl Schranz did well with his "patron" Kneissl; Nancy Greene became a top business woman and ski resort developer; and in the 1970's Austrian Annemarie Proell, who won three World Cups before she was twenty-one years old, was certain to exploit her fame when she retired. But to all of these champions, except Sailer who raced before there was a World Cup, despite huge commercial interests, winning the World Cup for what it meant—the best skier in the world—counted most of all.

Champions had to start young. Most of the world's top ski racers started skiing when they were three or four years old. American racers like Bobby Cochran, Mike Lafferty, Suzy Corrock, Cindy Nelson, the Cochran sisters, and other members of the U.S. ski team first got involved in local races. As they got older, they traveled to regional meets, entered divisional championships, then were noticed by ski association officials, entered junior championships, and did well enough to be selected for the national talent squad. Some time after that there was a breakthrough—a good performance during a big race where they beat skiers of standing. They were selected to attend one of the regional or possibly national training camps, where national team members were present to give them a point of comparison and bring them into contact with modern race techniques and top coaches. They moved up gradually, and some racers took longer than others because all persons do not develop—physically and mentally— at the same rate. With slight variations, national ski team members all over the world have gone through the same progression. It all adds up to the same thing: you have to climb up the ladder.

Let's look at how some members of the U.S. team got started on the road to becoming World Cup racers.

Mike Lafferty, a downhiller from Eugene, Oregon, talks about his experiences: "Skiing was always the one thing I really wanted to do. That was the one sport I was most excited about. I can't remember why. I started skiing when I was four or five. I can always remember that when the Warren Miller films came around, I would always be really excited. Initially, something got me really interested in skiing. It was something I wanted to do all the time. When I was ten, I idolized Buddy Werner, although I never really knew him. Then I started racing, and I did not always win races when I was young; but I did well enough. I used to fall a lot, but I always knew that I had the ability to do better. I kept working with it. I don't know exactly why, but I just wanted to do it. And now it is not the same as it was. I'm on a different level. There is a lot of difference between competing in college races and in World Cup races. When you start spending twelve months a year on it, which is basically what I'm doing and everyone else is also, it changes a lot. It's not the same sport. It's a profession.

"When I started, I raced in divisional races. I was nine or ten, and there was no real program at that time. I would just go to a race. The first program I was in was when I was fifteen. I skied then at Mount Bachelor, Oregon, and was coached by Frank Cammack, a really great coach who worked very hard and volunteered his services. I trained every Saturday and Sunday, ran slalom and giant slalom in the morning, and went to the races. Frank would show us different things, tell us what we were doing. He was one of the most important influences in my career.

"I stayed in that program until I went to college. In high school, skiing did not interfere with my school work. We would leave on a Thursday night, miss Friday, but never any extended periods. My limits were a couple of hundred miles. Nowadays, younger racers travel around the country while they are still in high school."

Cindy Nelson, from Lutzen, Minnesota, is a notable example of a racer who skied and studied at the same time. Cindy went to Europe for the first time in December, 1971, when she was sixteen years old. She was in high school and traveled the World Cup circuit with a case full of books: social studies, math, chemistry, and language manuals. Somehow or other between the tough training and racing schedules she found the time to study.

Cindy has dark eyes, long blonde hair, is five foot seven and a hefty 135 pounds. She is not typical of most U.S. racers in that she is from the Midwest. Back home, her grandfather owned a ski area, which her father managed. Cindy shussed and practiced the slalom, which was at first her strongest event. When she was a kid, the family went out to Colorado to ski during vacations. "My whole family skis—that's how I learned," she said in her midwestern accent. "A coach got me interested in racing and kind of brought me around, and we just free-skied. When I started racing more seriously, I would go race in some of the senior races in the mountains." Cindy Nelson was what the coaches call "a natural." When she was only fifteen, she placed fourth in the giant slalom and eighth in the downhill at the Junior National Championships, and rocketed onto the U.S. Ski Team.

Don Rowles, another member of the team, was born in Boise, Idaho, although he has lately been living in Sandy, Oregon. He started skiing when he was four and was racing at six all over Idaho. Then he joined the Mighty-Mites and continued to race. His parents paid the bills. At age thirteen, he became a junior racer, and in 1972 he was on the Can-Am circuit. Later that same year he went to Europe and participated in some European races, where he had good results for a first timer. Back home, he won the 1972 Can-Am trophy series, and in 1973, on his first World Cup circuit, he did fairly well in downhill.

Rowles is outspoken and expressive. He has graduated from high school and has temporarily given up going to college in order to train properly for the 1974 World Cup season and the World Championships at St. Moritz, Switzerland. "I plan to go on ski racing until I'm twenty-four or twenty-five," he said. "I may work into getting an education or go into the ski business. My folks are really cooperative, and I'm really fortunate that way. They just said that if I want to do this, they're behind me all the way. The whole works! They helped me in every way they could."

The support of her parents was also helpful to Suzy Corrock as she worked to become a champion racer. At the Sapporo, Japan, Olympic Games, Suzy won a bronze medal in the downhill, and that was clearly the most important moment in her career, which had, in a sense, started a decade earlier. "When the family went to Kitzbühel, Austria, for a year, I was ten and entered the school races. Father told my brother Ken that he could ski-race if he wanted to, and I just tagged along. My father was my only coach. Skiing for us was a family thing. Whatever I wanted to do with ski racing was my decision. When I was younger, if there was a course that was dangerous and I did not want to run it, it was always my decision whether I wanted to pull out, and I think that the reason I wasn't scared was because I had that decision. I always pushed myself a little bit harder. Mom and Dad feel that what I gained through ski racing I couldn't have gotten by going through life normally."

Suzy Corrock never took a ski lesson in her life. Most of the time she skied with her family. "As a kid, I admired a family friend named Jim Sweeney. He was a racer and quite a good one. One day, I really made progress in skiing by following him down Crystal Mountain. I had to ski very fast to keep up with him, and after that day, in every race I entered, my dad would tell me: 'Just follow Sweeney!' We all just enjoyed racing. It was fun."

Once a skier breaks out of the minor leagues and into the big time, his racing career becomes almost a year-round pursuit. Training U.S. racers for the World Cup circuit begins in the springtime. Ski racing, though, is basically an individual sport, and the team members live in all parts of the United States. Thus it is an expensive proposition to assemble them, and individual training programs are set up that can be carried on in the area of the country where the racers live. These programs are based on the needs of each racer—needs that have been determined by the previous season's results as well as by a careful study of the physical development of the individual involved. Some racers' programs may emphasize weight lifting, others long-distance running or bicycle riding and team sports.

Later on in the year, some team members may be sent to Chile for on-snow summer training, or to Australia and New Zealand, where they can race and perhaps improve their FIS point seedings. These seedings determine start positions in races and are particularly important in the slalom and giant slalom events. Generally, an earlier start means better snow conditions for the competitor. In September and October dry land training is organized in national camps, where the entire men's and women's teams come together. By November and December, on-snow camps are held in the new U.S. team training center at Park City, Utah.

That's the way training schedules are drawn up, but they don't always work out that way. Some team members have school or work obligations that prevent them from participating in certain training camps. Pressure is put on team members to participate in early season races when they would be better off training for the forthcoming season. Bad weather—rain, wind, fog, too much or not enough snow—can cause havoc in training camps. Shortage of funds can limit travel of team members, trainers, and coaches. So it often happens that although training programs are carefully planned, the scheduling is hard to maintain even though there is an important relationship between successful training camps and winning teams.

Just as each skier's training may vary in some ways from that of his teammates, every racer has his own personal style, technique, and approach to racing, and the individuality of U.S. team members is very evident as they talk about racing on the World Cup circuit.

After the season's first World Cup race in December, 1972, Mike Lafferty was talking about downhill at Val d'Isère, France, but he might have been back home in Oregon.

"I like going fast, I think; and there's a lot of things in downhill. It's just a neat feeling about going off bumps and flying. When you are working at going fast and are coming into a turn, you know you want to be on a certain line. You are going really fast and you want to make everything, do everything just right. It's really precise. You don't think about it very much while you are running the race because you have to be concentrating on everything at the same time. But when you go through a difficult section and do what you planned to do, like when you inspected the course the day before, you have a mental image of how you want to be standing, your position and where you want to be, and then if you come through going as fast as you can, you don't think about it—it's just a lot of fun."

The night before a race, Laff tries not to worry. Just before going to sleep, he thinks about the course, about the things he wants to do, about the way he wants to run the key sections. "That's what you have been doing all week, and you want to have yourself programmed well enough so that you just do it. I'm not very nervous before a race, just more single-minded. I'm trying to work myself into a condition where I am really concentrating on one thing."

On race day, he gets up at six-thirty and does exercises: sit-ups and push-ups to get the circulation going and the muscles loosened up. Then he goes outside to do some breathing exercises, jogs around, has breakfast, changes, picks up his training skis, and goes onto the course. "Just before the race I like to keep moving, keep physically nervous and loosened up."

Mike Lafferty is tall and thin, his head made rounder by his straight hair parted in the middle and plastered down on both sides. He has dark eyes, is good-looking, and is ranked among the ten best downhillers in the world. Having raced for a long time and developed his talents, he always has a good chance of winning a World Cup downhill. He placed third in the 1971 World Cup in the downhill specialty—the first American to have done so well. Top European downhillers like the Swiss Bernard Russi and Roland Collombin, the Austrian David Zwilling, and Frenchman Henri Duvillard respect Laff. His skiing style is very fluid, full of finesse; and when he is on the track, there is rarely a wasted movement to be detected.

During the 1973 season, however, Laff had a hard time getting himself together. Most of the time he concentrated on downhill. He had trouble with his equipment and changed skis many times. Even at that he placed ninth in two downhills at Garmisch, Germany, and his best placing was eighth in the Hahnenkamm at Kitzbühel.

In the Park Hotel in Wengen, Switzerland, Lafferty's teammate Don Rowles was talking about downhill: "There is a natural talent to ski flats. Sometimes I can ski them pretty well. I think I can do better here than I did at Garmisch, where the turns at the top were sheer ice. I'm from the Northwest, and we practically never have icy tracks. I have a basic problem of leaning in on ice and lifting my arm. They were high-speed icy turns, and we practically never got practice on those turns. If it was a soft course, I would have done better. I was raised in ruts three feet deep.

"On the circuit you go from area to area, and it is the same group of people everywhere. It can be depressing, but you think about racing and doing well. I know what I have to do, and I won't be satisfied until I do it. As amateurs we give everything we have for two and a half or three minutes each day, and that's it. Your way of life is organized to that way of thinking. You peak that much in a day and then you are backing off the rest of the day.

"Three days before the Garmisch race I was really psyched up. I was hyper. All I could think about was going fast. A guy gets psyched up and comes down at least six or seven times before a race. Maybe more, maybe ten times. The day before the Garmish race I was ready to go, then the day of the race I was really relaxed. I practiced yoga and concentrated on relaxing. You go off into a dream world that's not possible on the hill. An hour before the start, your mouth will dry out.

"The idea that you will fall always runs through your head, at least mine. You think: Well, you could fall here and that would be the end, hurt yourself, maybe be out for the season, maybe even kill yourself. It's possible. When you are riding in a car at seventy miles an hour and you look out the window and down at the ground, that's what you are doing on a pair of skis. Just imagine falling out of the car! But I don't mind falling because it makes me feel I can take a lot. I think, however, that if a guy let this get to him, it would ruin his downhill career.

"The idea of falling runs through your mind, though; then you concentrate on the course, then you just concentrate. You don't think about falling for very long. The adrenalin gets going, you get hyper, you are thinking of the course and a lot of people may be talking to you, but you are not really listening. The walkie-talkie radio reports where the course is bad, where to go wider or to cut in. When I get into the gate, all I want to do is to go fast. As far as line and all that, I can't really recall whether I remember where I've gone; I just go like crazy.

"You can't feel the speed, and you can't stop concentrating on the course to think. After you get through the finish gate, you realize it was fast, but when you are right on the course, none of these things comes into your mind. If they did, you would drop your concentration and maybe fall.

"Downhill is a great event that really challenges your body and mind. It's pretty difficult. You can see the blur of the people and the trees and your skis bouncing. I remember once that one ski crossed over the other when I was going seventy-five miles an hour! It just instantly bounced back. It's really a good feeling in downhill—like you have mastered yourself. In the slalom and giant slalom the feelings are completely different."

Cindy Nelson was billed as a downhiller when she went to Europe in 1971, although she has always insisted that she could run a good slalom and giant slalom as well. In her first race at St. Moritz on the World Cup circuit, she drew number 47. She placed thirteenth and beat "A" team members Marilyn and Barbara Cochran, not to mention fifty-two of the world's best downhillers. In her next race at Val d'Isère, with start number 69, she placed twelfth, and halfway down the course she had the sixth best time. Cindy was excited, but she was angry with herself for making so many mistakes. What she likes so much about the downhill is mastering the speed: "I try to be the master of the downhill course. Some downhills are really great. You know they have sharp turns and big bumps and are technically very difficult. Some people will back off and let the downhill take over. If you want to master it, turn in the right spot and stay on the line, you have to concentrate all the way down. You have time to think all the way down and ask, 'What should I be doing now?' I just love the speed, the turns, and going over the bumps—especially the bumps. If they have a sharp bump or something and I can take it smooth and only go off the ground a few inches or a few feet depending on the bump, that's the greatest feeling. When you're on the course, when you make a really good turn, it makes you feel really good. You just want to keep going and do it over and over again. It can feel really beautiful. When you make a bad turn, it kind of shakes you up.

"I've skied for a long time. I don't get sick of skiing. I just *love* it. Free skiing, racing, excitement—everything has a lot to do with it. Also, I feel that I have an ability to do it, a talent for it, and it is in my care to develop it as much as I can."

That year, in private, the coaches were saying that if any American girl was to win a downhill medal at the Sapporo Olympic Games, it would be Cindy Nelson. But Cindy was never to get to Japan. At Grindelwald, Switzerland, in the last downhill before the games, she made a mistake. Disaster followed. "The day of the race I was carrying more speed than I had in training. I came down the chute and just did not think, missed my timing, and just could not pull out of the fall." Cindy hit the *piste* so hard that she broke her hip and spent fifteen days of pain in a Swiss hospital. That was just the beginning of a six-month period of convalescence. She returned to high school on crutches. Her hip healed perfectly. She began walking again, but her knees bothered her. She did some light jogging, played some tennis, finished her junior year, and during summer vacation played a lot of softball and water-skied.

She was admitted to the national training camp at Bend, Oregon, in September, where she skied some slalom, and by December she was back in Europe at Val d'Isère. She had done little downhill training, and her race time showed it. Instead of ending up among the first fifteen racers as she had the previous year, she finished thirtieth. After the race she explained her performance by saying that she, like the rest of the team, had had very little downhill practice, implying that in the later season downhills her times and standing would improve.

It was not to be. Cindy did not get the chance to race in any more European World Cup events that year. In the middle of December, the United States Ski Association was forced to slash its budget, and the Alpine racing program was seriously curtailed. Newly hired coaches were fired, and Hank Tauber, who had been assistant head of the Alpine program, resigned. Schedules and priorities were shifted. A lot of people were shocked, disappointed, and disillusioned. Men's coach Hans Peter Rohr traveled around most of the World Cup circuit without an assistant. He had to go to meetings, train the racers, wax their skis, and do most of the menial work. Other teams had managers who took care of all the details and a coach who did nothing but coach. Besides Rohr, a lot of people were asking how it was that one of the richest countries in the world did not have enough pride and interest in ski racing to support its teams financially. They were asking how it was possible to set up a program that looked beautiful on paper and then not support it?

What other people were saying, the racers were feeling. Cindy Nelson and Susie Patterson, another team member, were among the worst hit. Anxious to participate in the January and February World Cup events, Cindy and Susie privately raised enough money to pay their way to the Maribor, Yugoslavia, World Cup slalom meeting, but when they arrived, they were told that ski association officialdom back in Denver had prohibited them from racing. A lot of reasons were given, but the girls finally concluded that they were the victims of a struggle for authority in the association itself.

Defeated in politics and personally depressed, the girls returned to the States. "I would have quit a long time ago if I didn't enjoy racing so much," Cindy said in an interview in the Denver paper, *Ski Racing*. "I really like skiing and racing, and quitting would put it out of my life." But the consequences of her non-participation in the European World Cup downhills and other events were serious. Cindy was given no chance to improve her seeding, so important in the giant slalom and in the slalom; and she was pushed out of the first seed in the downhill by up and coming racers.

During the rest of the 1973 winter Cindy raced on the Can-Am circuit and worked hard to improve her slalom and giant slalom technique. She felt that she had good potential in those events as well as in the downhill. When the United States "A" team came back from Europe for the United States National Championships, Cindy was ready. In the downhill she beat the field, including Suzy Corrock, who had won a bronze medal at Sapporo. "I didn't have a perfect run," she said. "You never have a perfect race when you're winning. You're going too fast for that."

Barbara Ann Cochran won an Olympic gold medal in the slalom at Sapporo; she and sister Marilyn won a silver medal in the slalom and a bronze medal in the combined at the Val Gardena, Italy, World Championships in 1970; Marilyn won a World Cup in the giant slalom in 1969, and together they have won fifty or sixty top places in World Cup races during the past eight years.

In 1972, Marilyn who was born in 1949 and attends the University of Vermont, had a disappointing Olympic season; but she came back in 1973, after very little training, to place well in several World Cup events. She won the Chamonix, France, Kandahar slalom, the giant slalom in Naeba, Japan (where she beat World Cup holder Annemarie Proell), and in several of the early downhills placed among the top ten finishers. "This year," she said when I talked with her at Grindelwald, Switzerland, "I'm trying to organize my thoughts and my head. I don't feel I am a very good ski racer yet because of the way I approach ski racing. Technically, I ski well enough to be great, but a lot of girls do that. The great ones organize their mental condition as well." Marilyn is working hard to win the World Cup in 1974 and perhaps a medal at the St. Moritz World Championships. "Right now, ski racing has provided more of a human than a physical development. Two or three years ago athletic development was more important. I'm not strong enough at present to chop off my career. When the going gets a little tough, I just don't want to quit, just say, well that's it. I expect to continue through the 1974 World Championships. In the meantime, I'm trying to learn more self-control."

One of Marilyn's main problems up until now has been her slowness of getting into top form. Her best performances inevitably have come toward the end of the competition season. The World Championships, like the Olympic Games, are staged in February.

Marilyn's sister Barbara Ann, whose career peaked with her slalom gold medal at Sapporo, can see the time when World Cup racing will no longer be a part of her life. She is studying liberal arts at the University of Vermont, and attending college seriously interfered with her training during the 1973 season. Her aim is to be a more consistent ski racer. She believes that she can improve a great deal in downhill, which is her weakest event, and she has to get her "timing down" in giant slalom. "Ski racing," she said, "is pretty important right now, but not as much as before. I wouldn't want to quit right now, but I can see the time when I will quit."

In 1973 she placed fifth in the Grindelwald slalom, ninth in the Chamonix Kandahar slalom, ninth in the giant slalom at Abetone, Italy, fifth in the slalom at Mont Saint-Anne, Canada, and her best season's performance was a third place in the Naeba, Japan, slalom.

The Cochran sisters have been the mainstays of the women's team for many years. During the 1973–74 season they will be racing against tough Austrian, French, German, and Swiss women: three-time World Cup winner Annemarie Proell, her teammate Monika Kaserer, the German slalom great Rosi Mittermaier, the French trio Jacqueline Rouvier, Danièle Debernard, and Patricia Emonet, the Swiss double gold medalist Marie-Theres Nadig, and outsiders like the Lichtenstein girl Hanny Wenzel, as well as other U.S. team members who are hungry for titles and world recognition. In what will probably be their final season on the team, Marilyn and Barbara Ann will be pitting their experience and racing maturity against all of these contenders.

Of all the members of the United States men's team, twenty-two-year-old Bobby Cochran—the brother of Marilyn and Barbara Ann—is the most versatile. He is a threat to the world's best in the downhill and the slalom, and if he works on his giant slalom technique, he will be a true three-event threat—a rare combination in World Cup competition. During the 1973 season he had moments of brilliance—a third place in the Hahnenkamm downhill, a first in the combined, and a first place in the Heavenly Valley World Cup giant slalom—mixed with lapses where he finished in the second and third seeds. Despite this, he is the finest ski racer in the United States. At Jackson Hole, Wyoming, he swept the United States National Championships with first places in the downhill, the slalom, and the giant slalom. Moreover, his approach to ski racing is extremely serious, and he is probably the most intellectual ski racer who has ever existed. For 1974 Bobby will be in top physical condition and a definite threat for the FIS World Championships.

Bobby Cochran, with his analytical mind, is a new breed of ski racer. He is meticulous in his study of racecourses, and he is able to adapt his techniques to the demands of the track and the weather. At present he is one of the disappearing brand of ski racers who believes he can race and continue his education at the same time. "I didn't go into college with the idea that I would get done in four years," said Bobby in an interview at Wengen, Switzerland. "I figured it would take six, seven years. I wanted to go to school. My folks said that education was important, but they also said that ski racing itself was an education. I think that you can put off college, where you cannot put off ski racing. This is the time to do ski racing if you are going to do it."

Bobby's intellectual and analytical abilities combine best when he talks about ski racing and, in particular, the downhill. "I think of turns, and I would like to make very, very precise turns like a figure skater does in the school figures—at any speed, anywhere. I'm getting to that point, but at high speeds I'm not really doing that. I want every turn I make, whether I'm off balance or not, to be carved, carved completely, all the way around.

"A perfectly carved turn means that at the beginning of the turn you bend your ski at an arc, and the tip of the ski or edge makes a groove in the snow, and in a perfect turn the rest of the ski would follow in that groove all the way around, without any sliding from that groove. You try to make turns as close to that ideal as possible. I can feel if my skis are flat or are slipping. Sometimes you will be good at the beginning of the turn and feel the edge making a very smooth arc, and then at the end of the turn you may slide or chatter—not so much during a race as in free skiing. On a slow course you are more aware of it; not so much on an icy course."

Preoccupied with the struggle for precision at high speed, Bobby Cochran has reached a point in his technical and physical development where it is possible for him to strive for perfection. After a poor, unexplainable performance in the Wengen downhill, he said: "Before a downhill race you get sort of wired up almost. You have to keep that down, at least I do, or you get too jumpy and you cannot make precise controlled muscle movements. Slalom is a little different, but in downhill you have to be very controlled and strong on your skis. I concentrate on what I have to do in the

downhill. How to make the turns, line, and everything. I try to
concentrate on details and not on the race itself. I have some fear,
but not of physical harm, more worry about what is going to happen in the race, how you are going to do. It's sort of tied in with
being wired up—always trying to be very relaxed but having my
muscles toned, not jumpy. Right before the start, say thirty seconds,
I try to do some exercises, some jumping up and down.

"On the course I have a feeling of trying to drive forward, a
feeling of controlling the course. During the first couple of training
runs the course pretty much controls you. Then, through every run,
you learn more and more about the course until you come to the
point where you feel you control it. Then there is this feeling of
driving down the mountain—it's trying to attack the course which
is in the front of your mind. You just want to tear it apart, like
that's in the front of your mind. But in the back, in the sub-
conscious, you are telling your muscles to get low, get your arms
way in front, press bumps. If you don't have any idea of how to
attack it, you are sunk.

"After the race today I felt frustrated, had this feeling that I
did what I wanted to do but I just did not figure out this course. I
was not fast in training. I wasn't pressing the bumps well enough.
You can feel that you are pressing the bumps, but you aren't
pressing, particularly in a straight section, on little dips about a foot
high. In the depressions if you unweight on the front side and press
down on the back side, you get acceleration. That way you run
across a flat much faster. But the timing is very critical. You
have to start the movements early, even if unconsciously. Many
turns in ski racing are made unconsciously. I don't want to get
wrapped up in the winning or losing. A racer has to prepare himself to ski the course faster than the other guy, or rather to ski
the course as fast as he possibly can. When he does that, he
has achieved his object really. At the same time, I don't think you
should get too involved in just the pure aspects of ski racing."

That was at Wengen, Switzerland, after the downhill, which was
held at Grindelwald, a few miles away. Bobby had finished in
twenty-second place, four seconds off Swiss winner Bernard Russi's
time. The team moved over to Megève, France, where Bobby

placed tenth in the slalom. Then the caravan packed up skis and suitcases and drove through the Mont Blanc tunnel, across northern Italy, over the Brenner Pass and into Kitzbühel, Austria—the home of Toni Sailer and many other Austrian greats—for the Hahnen-kamm race on the toughest downhill *piste* in the world: the Streif.

After the race, in a hotel room cluttered with clothing, helmets, half-emptied suitcases, casette recorders, books, and the rest of a ski racer's paraphernalia, Bobby Cochran talked about what happened there. He speaks in a careful voice, something like a doctor analyzing a patient's illness, only the patient happens to be the track and the man who ran it: "I got a good start. I poled out of the start well and could feel it. I poled all the way through like a cross-country skier. I felt like I went through the gate really fast. In the first turn, I got a little bit low, but I made sure I kept my skis carving and not sliding. On the *Mausfalle* [a steep wall] I flew a little bit, more that I have been, but I got right into my tuck and I carried my speed, and then there is a very hard right-hand turn just before the Steilhang [a steep pitch]. I went into it O.K. I should have gone into it better. Especially at the end of the turn I leaned in, and there is a drop-off at the gate just as you are finishing your turn. It's not a good idea to lean in there —you want to stay right over your skis—and the best way is to press down on the bump. I leaned in and finished part of the turn on my uphill ski and got my downhill ski back under me. And it just didn't make a good turn. I think I was just a hair late because I was thinking of pressing a bump. I was concentrating so hard on that that I was maybe a little late for the turn, wasn't ready enough. Lost time there.

"I was concerned with making sure I skied right. I hadn't been skiing well before; but I knew what I had to do. I wanted to be very aware, very sensitive to what my skis were doing, and I wanted to be feeling every little bump—you know how they were biting into the snow, whether they were slipping a little bit. You can usually feel that, whether your tails are sliding out. If you are conscious of what your skis are doing beneath your feet, then you are aware of this and can correct it. It's like you have an eye

Toni Sailer, winner of three gold medals at the Cortina Olympics, races in the slalom near Vienna in 1957.

Office National Autrichien du Tourisme, Paris

The late Buddy Werner *(left)* receives congratulations from Bob Beattie, former coach of the U.S. Olympic team, in Innsbruck in 1963.

Del Mulkey

Jean-Claude Killy, the French Wor[ld] and Olympic champion, entered one of his first ski races at the age [of] six.

Robert Killy

World Cup champion Jean-Clau[de] Killy *(left)* shared the spotlight w[ith] Karl Schranz after the Austrian's 19th victory in the downhill race at V[al] d'Isère, France.

Harvey Edwa[rds]

Harvey Edwards

arl Schranz skis to victory in the
971 Hahnenkamm downhill in Kitz-
ühel, Austria, his last race as an
mateur.

1968, Nancy Greene and Jean-
laude Killy were each awarded the
orld Cup—the second time both ski-
rs had won the coveted prize.

Bernard Cahier-Evian

Thousands of ski enthusiasts come to Kitzbühel, Austria, every year to see the Hahnenkamm races, one of the classic meets in World Cup competition.

Former U.S. coach Ron Sargent *(right)* helps prepare skis before the season's first race at Val d'Isère, France.

arvey Edwards   *Harvey Edwards*

Harvey Edwards   *Harvey Edwards*

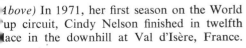

Above) In 1971, her first season on the World 'up circuit, Cindy Nelson finished in twelfth lace in the downhill at Val d'Isère, France.

Right) Don Rowles takes to the air during a ownhill race at St. Moritz, Switzerland, in 'hich he took tenth place.

(Left) Marilyn Cochran skis the sl
lom in the World Cup race at S
Gervais, France, in 1973, one of h
most successful seasons.

(Opposite page, top) Bobby Cochra
shown here in both the downhill ar
slalom races at St. Moritz, Switzerlan
was the top U.S. contender in bo
events.

(Below) Barbara Ann Cochran
mobbed by her teammates after h
gold medal victory in the slalom at tl
Sapporo, Japan, Olympic Games
1972.

Harvey Edwards   *Harvey Edwards*

Harvey Edwards   Harvey Edwards   Harvey Edwards   Harvey Edwards

U.S. skiers face stiff competition from European champions such as Switzerland's Bernard Russi *(above)* and three-time World Cup winner Annemarie Proell of Austria *(right)*.

As many as 10,000 skiers start the 85-kilometer (53-mile) Vasaloppet Race in Norway, making it the largest cross-country race in the world.

(*Left*) Sixten Jernberg of Sweden dominated Nordic skiing from 1954 until 1964, winning many Olympic and World Championship medals.

(*Opposite page, top*) John Bower, the only American to win a major cross country race, is congratulated by Norway's King Olaf V on his victory in the 1968 Holmenkollen King's Cup.

(*Opposite page, bottom left*) Martha Rockwell, the best woman cross-country racer in the U.S., runs the 10-kilometer event at Falun, Sweden.

(*Opposite page, bottom right*) Although eighteen-year-old Tim Caldwell finished sixteenth in this race at Falun, he went on to place second in the 15-kilometer junior event at Holmenkollen.

(*Below*) A jumper seems to hang in the air after a leap from the 70-meter hill used in the Nordic combined ski jumping events.

Knut Edv. Holm

Harvey Edwards

Bob and Ira Spring
Harvey Edwards

Harvey Edwards
Harvey Edwards

Right and below) Climbing skins dry in the sun outside a cabin in the Italian Alps, while inside ski tourers enjoy companionship and a hot meal.

Harvey Edwards   *Harvey Edwards*

In northern Italy a lone skier mak[es] his way up a trail that leads to a h[ut]

Harvey Edwards

Booming through the light powder an[d] reacting to every bump and change [of] direction are what every skier drea[ms] about all year long.

the High Route from Chamonix,
ance, to Zermatt, Switzerland, this
er will experience the pleasures of
itude and adventure that make ski
uring a welcome change from city
e.

Harvey Edwards

All skiers from beginners to experts look to the champions in their efforts to go farther, faster, and better.

almost on your feet. You want to be that sensitive, you want to be able to feel everything as if you have extrasensory perception. I try to do that. You are using the nerves in your feet, and you can build up a very delicate sensitive system of nerves so that you can feel your skis.

"The Streif is the most difficult downhill course in the world. It is tough because of the high-speed turns, the very high speeds you hit, the many different skills that are required to run it. At the top you have a couple of very, very wide fast turns, which take one sort of technique; you have very, very icy fallaway traverses with bumps on them, which take other skills. Riding bumps takes a lot of skill. Then you have the roads, which take another kind of skill; then you have *Hausburg,* which combines a lot of things— bumps, which are very difficult to get; the long fallaway turn, which is fast; the finish, which is almost like the speed trials at Cervinia, Italy. You are going straight down on that very steep hill for a long ways, and after you get going over eighty miles per hour, you have a very sharp transition at the end of it, and then you drop, down into the finish. On that final schuss I could have tucked better, but I was working very hard on pressing the bumps."

In the downhill, Bobby Cochran finished third and the following day did well enough in the slalom to win the Hahnenkamm combined trophy—the first American to win this honor.

3

CROSS-COUNTRY RACING

Although John A. (Snowshoe) Thomson was delivering mail on skis to gold rush miners for twenty years in the Sierra Nevada Mountains of California in the 1850's, cross-country skiing or ski touring in the United States did not really become popular until about a hundred years later. Actually, skiing had been introduced earlier to Canada, around 1725, and professional ski races—organized by Norwegians—were held on downhill courses in California in the 1870's.

In Scandinavia, however, people were skiing some four thousand years ago. Ski touring was and still is a means of transportation and pleasure—an integral part of the Scandinavian way of life. Being competitive people, the Finns, Norwegians, and Swedes refined the sport, improved techniques and equipment, and for the elite and an excited public established Nordic "classic" races like the Holmenkollen in Norway, the Swedish Ski Games in Sweden, and the Lahti Games in Finland. By far, the Scandinavians have had the greatest influence on cross-country racing, an influence that has affected the recreational aspects of the sport throughout the world. The fact that cross-country skiing is deeply rooted in the customs and traditions of Scandinavian life, while it is just another sport in North America, only partially explains why so many Finns, Norwegians, and Swedes have been great cross-country ski racers and why so few have been Americans.

Since World War II, the Russians, Poles, East and West Germans, Italians, Swiss, Czechs, and Japanese have produced champion racers and jumpers, who moved in on the Scandinavian domination. At Innsbruck in 1964, a Swiss won the 15-kilometer combined event, a German won the combined ski jump, Russian women won the 5-kilometer, 10-kilometer, and relay races; at Grenoble four years later, an Italian won the 30-kilometer race, a German won the combined race-jump championship, a Czech won the 70-meter jump, and a Russian won the 90-meter jump. At Sapporo in 1972, an East German won the combined, Russians won the 30-kilometer, the men's cross-country and biathlon relays, and the three women's races, a Pole won the 90-meter jump, and the Japanese swept the 70-meter jump. No American, however, has ever won a medal at a Nordic World Ski Championship or the Olympic Games, and only a handful of Americans have ever done well or won major races at international ski meets.

Many explanations, official and otherwise, have been given: lack of money to establish complete programs, inadequate coaching, the lack of quality races in the United States and Canada, even the American way of life—dependent on the automobile and easy living. It was claimed that American life did not help build the tough, rugged men and women needed in a sport dependent on endurance. It was also pointed out that the Scandinavian "amateur" racers were paid prize money or given objects of value that could and were converted to money, while American cross-country racers, if they were lucky, had a scholarship at a university. Once they finished their schooling, the necessities of making a living for themselves, and possibly their families, prevented them from training properly and continuing their careers.

Many of these are valid reasons for our failure in past years to field winning cross-country teams. Recently, however, things have been getting better. Training conditions in the United States are better organized, and foreign racers have been invited to compete in North American races, thus providing the best example to prospective American racers of what top competition is all about. The ski industry's support of cross-country racing and a more enlightened coaching program, which now draws on a far wider base of competitors because of the increased interest in cross-country skiing in elementary schools, high schools, and colleges—all these factors have done much to beef up the United States program. Many of the reasons or excuses used in the past to explain American failure to do well are gradually disappearing. More than ever before, American cross-country competitors have the potential and the will to win. It cannot yet be claimed that we have a team of depth and are seriously challenging the Scandinavians and others at their game, but if the interest in cross-country skiing and racing continues to grow in the United States, we soon will be in the position of overseas challenger.

One of the greatest cross-country racers of all time was the Swede Sixten Jernberg, who was known for his tremendous strength. Jernberg or "Iron Mountain" lived up to his name. He was a tough lumberjack, a woodsman. From 1954 until 1964 he dominated three Olympic Games, two Nordic World Championships, and almost every race he entered.

Jernberg was born in 1929 at Limedsforsen, about 250 miles north of Stockholm. He was selected for the Swedish national team in 1954 and placed fourth in the 30-kilometer world championship race at Falun. That year at Oslo's Holmenkollen, he won the 15-kilometer event and placed second in the 50-kilometer. By 1955, Jernberg was on top. Successively, he won the 30-kilometer race at Cortina and Moscow, the 85.6-kilometer Vasaloppet—the longest international ski marathon in the world—and two out of three events at the Swedish championships. The following year, in his first Olympic Games, Jernberg won a gold in the 50, a silver in the 15- and 30-kilometer races, and a bronze for his leg in the 4 × 10 kilometer relay event.

From then on he and the Finn Veikko Hakulinen ruled the world's cross-country tracks as a pair of racers had never done before. When the Nordic World Championships were held in Lahti, Finland, in 1958, Jernberg proved once again to be a phenomenal athlete. Jernberg's supporters were at first disappointed by a fourth place in the 15-kilometer race; but in the 50-kilometer event he beat Hakulinen by more than a minute for a gold medal.

He then led the relay team to another gold when he finished the first leg with an eighteen-second lead over his adversary.

Throughout his career, Jernberg won fifteen gold, thirteen silver, and seven bronze medals in the Swedish championships, and he won the Vasaloppet marathon six times straight.

Mike Brady, one of skiing's most knowledgeable Nordic experts, has written of Jernberg: "Jernberg's secret lay literally in his will to compete. In 1960, for instance, he entered 35 races in four months, racing a total distance of 790.5 kilometers. In these races he took 19 gold, 6 silver, 6 bronze medals, 10 fourth places, and 5 fifth places; an average placing of 1.94. He won all the Swedish championship races, took two Olympic medals in Squaw Valley, won the Vasaloppet, Norway's super-tough Monolitt Park race (a 15-kilometer "sprint"), and won again on the fast tracks in the Kiruna games in northern Sweden.

"Jernberg's iron will was matched by his sheer strength and phenomenal endurance. In spite of these characteristics, he had an almost happy-go-lucky approach to racing that sometimes unnerved the competition. He loved the tough races: the more brutal the hills, the more he liked them—like his own tracks in the woods of Lima. He mastered all the distances, from 10 kilometer sprints to the 85.6-kilometer-long Vasaloppet."

In 1964, rumor had it that Jernberg's strength was finally failing, and some people even claimed that the Swede—never known for his technique—feared the smooth-flowing powerful style of the Finn Eero Mäntryranta. This seemed to be confirmed when Jernberg took it easy during the early season races. But he came to the Innsbruck Olympics and poured it on once again. He placed third in the 15-kilometer race, beaten by Mäntyranta and Norway's Harald Grönningen. In the 30-kilometer race, he was a disappointing fifth. But in the 50 he beat Mäntryranta by a healthy four minutes to place first. In addition, he helped Sweden win the gold medal in the 4 × 10 kilometer relay.

After ten years on the competition scene, Jernberg retired to his farm in Lima, which subsequently expanded to become an athletic and recreation center. By then Hakulinen had also quit, and a great era of cross-country racing had come to an end.

Unlike Jernberg, America's John Bower won just one important race, but it was the highlight of his career and marked a turning point in cross-country competition for the United States. Bower's win proved once and for all that Americans, given the devotion, will power, and proper training, could successfully compete against the world Nordic elite.

The Holmenkollen Nordic combined championships, which Bower won in 1968 to receive the King's Cup, is Nordic skiing's oldest and most coveted award. The cup was first awarded in 1879 on the Huseby Hill outside of Oslo. At that time each competitor leaped off the jump, went immediately onto the cross-country track that led up to the jump again, and leaped once more. The competitor with the best style and shortest total time was declared the winner. This event, in modified form, became known as the Nordic combined. Today it consists of two events, if possible held on separate days: a 15-kilometer run and jumping, usually on a 70-meter hill. The results of both events are calculated, and the competitor with the most points is declared Nordic combined champion.

Up until 1933, the Nordic combined was the only event at Norway's Holmenkollen. Then special jumping and running events were added, until the Holmenkollen meeting assumed greater importance in Nordic lands than the Olympic Games. The Holmenkollen is to Scandinavia what the World Series or Super Bowl games are to the United States. Schools and factories close, work stops, holidays are declared, and crowds of 75,000 to 100,000 people, many of them on foot, walk up to Oslo's Nordmarka Park to watch the great skiers and jumpers in action. One of the major problems of the organizers is to keep avid cross-country skiers from getting onto the tracks to practice their style and endurance behind their heroes and heroines. Among cross-country racers and jumpers Holmenkollen winners are more highly regarded than Olympic champions. At the Olympics the number of competitors are limited to four per event from each country; at the Holmenkollen, the total number of entrants is often larger. That means that the competition from Scandinavia, Eastern, and Central Europe is tougher, and most of the winners come from those countries.

The Nordic combined events require not only endurance but also versatility. Often a competitor may either be a good jumper or a good cross-country runner—rarely both at the same time—but the key to winning the Nordic combined is to perfect these two skills so that the competitor is a contender in both. The jumping and running events are decidedly different. Running is for lean endurance athletes who must keep moving mile after mile. Jumping is mastered by the more quick gymnastic type who puts all into a leap and flight lasting only a few seconds. Thus, training for the Nordic combined presents particular problems equivalent to training for both the shot put and the marathon in track and field. The question facing combined coaches is how to mix the two types of training necessary for these events so that a competitor comes to his peak during the competition season.

It was while working with John Bower that the head United States cross-country coach Al Merrill (who became Nordic combined coach in 1973) found that it was virtually impossible to train intensively in both events at the same time. He decided that the best way for a Nordic combined skier to train was to work hardest on his weakest event and keep up a maintenance program in the other. Bower, who was born in Maine, was a good Alpine racer, and when he decided in college to specialize in Nordic skiing, he applied downhill techniques on downhill sections of cross-country tracks. Merrill, therefore, worked on Bower's jumping—his weakest event.

John Bower became a member of the national team in 1962, and in 1964 he was sent to Europe for early season intensive jumping training with the regular jumpers from the U.S. team. Coach Merrill firmly believed that Bower had the potential to be one of the top ten Nordic combined men in the world. At the Innsbruck Olympics, Bower placed ninth in the 15-kilometer race and twenty-first in the 70-meter jump, for an overall placing of fifteenth—a respectable performance.

Four years later, when he was twenty-eight, Bower decided that 1968 would be his final season on the U.S. team. For him the purpose of ski racing was never just to strive to win. It was a means to physical development and the building of character; and by then he felt he had gone about as far as he could. In 1968 he geared himself for his final season and trained very hard.

With each race he got better. In the Nordic combined at the Grenoble Olympic games, he placed thirteenth behind the German Franz Keller. At the Lahti games in Finland he was ninth; at the Swedish games he placed second. Then came the Holmenkollen on March 14, 1968. John Bower, with start number 33, was the last Nordic combined racer to start. The 15-kilometer course was icy and hard, but Bower, having been brought up in Maine, liked that, particularly the downhill sections, which he often ran outside of the "rails" to pick up more speed. He was also favored by his start number. He started just thirty seconds behind the 1967 Holmen-kollen and 1968 Olympic champion Franz Keller. For two years Keller had beaten Bower in every race in which they met, so Bower knew that if he could catch the German and pass him, he would be thirty seconds ahead. Keller was good on the flats and going up hills; Bower was good on the hills and going down them.

When Bower caught Keller about five kilometers from the start, he knew that victory was in sight. He poured it on and passed him. He galloped up the hills and sunk into the aerodynamic egg position of the Alpine racer in the downhill sections—to win the cross-country part of the Nordic combined by twelve seconds.

Two days later the jumping event was held on the Holmenkollen hill, where Bower had never placed better than twelfth. He was given very little chance to win the combined. But he was up for the event. Had he not been getting better all season long? Had he not waited six years for this, his last big fling in international competition? He needed two good jumps. "His first jump," recalled Al Merrill, "was a long one—over 80 meters and in fine style. That put him into first place and gave him a psychological ad-vantage over the competition. They just could not match it." John Bower eventually finished fourth in the jumping competition to win the Holmenkollen Nordic combined. He had achieved the difficult feat of being strong in both cross-country running and jumping at the same time. According to *Skiing International Yearbook 1969,* when he was handed the King's Cup by Norway's King Olav V,

Bower said: "This was my last race. Who would have thought it would be the most exciting?"

Until the middle 1960's the number of women cross-country racers in the United States was very low. American women did not seem to be interested, the idea was not accepted by society, and it was thought that women were too soft to compete in a sport that demanded a particularly punishing kind of training. Then in 1969, a short, lithe, dark-complexioned woman of twenty-four named Martha Rockwell was sent to Durango, Colorado, by the eastern division of the United States Ski Association. Her coach, Tom Upham, thought Martha would have a chance in the national Nordic championships, and Martha, who did not know anything about the competition she would encounter the first year women's senior races were held, was willing to try anything, at least once. Upham worried because Martha had never trained at the higher western altitudes, and he thought that would slow her down. Not Martha, though. "No one knew who I was," she said. "I just showed up, brown corduroys and all. I didn't know anything. I just started and ran as fast as I could and did not stop until I got back again. I won . . . everything."

That was the Jim Thorpe beginning of the career of America's finest woman cross-country racer, who proved during the 1973 season that she was a serious challenge to the world's best.

Where, though, did she come from, how did she get interested in what was then a way-out sport, and why? These were some of the questions that were raised after the U.S. Nationals. Actually, Martha Rockwell started to ski when she was four, and by the 1960's when she attended the Putney School in Putney, Vermont, she subconsciously wanted to be a racer. At that time, however, it was thought unseemly for American women to run cross-country. Once a year there were inter-class races, where the principal role of the girls was to pack out the track for the boys and hand them orange segments during the races. After Putney, Martha attended Bennington College, but the atmosphere in both school and college was not conducive to producing competitive skiers. After graduating from college, she went to work for a few years in New York

City in the graphic arts field, then moved back up to New England, where she worked for small book publishers.

In the winter of 1968, Martha returned to Putney to visit her mother and noticed that some girls were skiing cross-country. She spoke with Sweden's Olympic gold medal winners Barbro Martinsson and Toini Gustafsson, who had come to a nearby race to encourage American girls to take up the sport. Martha liked what they said and began training on her own.

She was living and working in Boston at the time, and she would get up early in the morning and run in a park near her apartment. After work, she would drive twenty-five miles out of town to a small ski area. She would put on her skis and run a fast sprint to get her heart up to 180 or 200 beats per minute; then after a short rest, she would run another sprint. Called interval training, it is particularly useful for cross-country racers, who encounter flat sections followed by climbs, followed by downhill sections on which the skier can rest. Interval training builds up the capacity to tolerate oxygen debt in what is otherwise considered an endurance event. Thus it is vital to hill running in cross-country—and hills are often where races are won and lost.

June, 1970, a year after she made the team, Martha was sent to Sweden. In her first international competition—a 5-kilometer race —Martha was about five minutes behind the winner's time. "It was just ridiculous," she said. "In today's races if you are two minutes out, you are way out of it." The Scandinavian trip, though, was not a complete failure. While there, she learned what real training was all about, and she realized how far behind she was. She reasoned that being older and more mature than many of the Scandinavians and American racers gave her an advantage. She was able to concentrate more intensely. She also figured that had she become interested in cross-country when she was younger, she would have gotten caught in the major technique changes of the 1950's and 1960's. So being older was no great handicap. Were there not women on the Russian and Finnish teams who were over thirty and still winning races? Martha's goal was clear: she wanted to progress to a point where she would be in a position to challenge the Scandinavians and Russians who were dominating the women's events.

Back at Putney, John Caldwell, who at the time was head coach of the U.S. teams and a teacher in the school, and Bob Gray, one of the veteran American racers, helped her establish a training program. Martha took to the routines quickly. At heart, she was a loner, and cross-country racing—striding through the woods, galloping up hills, schussing down, going off into the woods again—against time and the competition satisfied her personality needs. Besides that, it was about the only competitive sport that she could have started so late in life.

During the early spring she rode her bicycle three to four hours a day; this increased to five to six hours during the summer months. "I just love to train," she said. "And I love the actual race as well. What I like about racing is the challenge, the idea that the day after tomorrow at ten-thirty I've got to be right on that line and ready to go, and all the training I have done since last May somehow has to be focused in on that moment, and then I have five or ten kilometers just to utilize and focus that energy. When I started cross-country skiing, I continued because of that aspect. That really is exciting, if all goes well."

Martha was sent to the Sapporo Olympics in 1972 and turned in the best performance of any American female. In the 5-kilometer race she finished eighteenth, just fifty seconds off the time of top Russian Galina Koulacova; in the 10-kilometer event she finished sixteenth, a little over two minutes back. Martha believed that she could have done much better. "Martha is not a natural," said Marty Hall, coach of the ladies' cross-country teams. "She was made by herself. Martha is negative, works off a negative base. She gets 'down' after a bad race, and it is hard for her to get 'up' again."

Martha went back to Putney and in the spring began a new training program. In the past she had trained until she was exhausted. She wasn't the sort of person who organized her training scientifically. And besides that, in the United States there had always been a great deal of controversy about whether greater emphasis should be placed on interval or distance training. Marty Hall, who had in the meantime taken over as head coach of the cross-country teams, suggested that she should work with weights, not so much for building muscles as to give her more flexibility. She rode her bicycle, did some skiing on roads with special roller skis, raced up hills with her ski poles, and ran in the woods.

It was in October, while running interval loops on foot in the woods, that Martha Rockwell's cross-country career almost came to an end. She stumbled on a loose rock and fell badly. She pulled all the ligaments in her ankle. For a month her ankle was in a cast, and her training was interrupted. She whiled away the days by lifting weights, to build up her upper body.

At the beginning of the 1973 season, Martha Rockwell was more or less ready. At Bohinj, Yugoslavia, she won her first race; the following week at Castelrotto Ronzone, Italy, she won again, and ten days later at Reit-im-Winkl, Germany, she placed third, only twenty seconds off the winner's time. All races had international participation and, as Marty Hall said, Martha had her season made.

In the Scandinavian "classic" races she had moderate results, her best being a seventh place in the 5-kilometer event and a sixth place in the 10-kilometer races at Norway's Holmenkollen. She was still behind some of the Finns and Russians, but she beat several Olympic and world champion skiers. Martha said: "My goal is to achieve a level of technical perfection and a background of endurance, to be among the top group. I don't look forward so much to winning, but being there and being in a position to win, if the good day comes."

Cross-country racing for men is much more firmly established in the United States than that for women. Despite this (and with the exception of John Bower), there have been few great male cross-country racers. Tim Caldwell, a student at Dartmouth College and a member of the cross-country team, is a fine prospect. Caldwell had practically the opposite background from Martha Rockwell. They were united only in their fondness for developing their bodies and minds through training and racing to win.

Tim Caldwell was a natural athlete. He grew up in an atmosphere where cross-country skiing was a way of life. His father, a member of the 1952 Olympic team and for many years head coach of the United States team, encouraged him to ski. The family lived at

Putney, Vermont, where Mr. Caldwell wrote books about cross-country skiing, taught math, and coached skiing, soccer, and baseball. Tim began to ski when he was two or three years old. He skied while going to elementary school, but at that time he favored the Alpine over the cross-country events.

In high school, influenced somewhat by his father, Tim began to take cross-country racing seriously. He was talented and had a good attitude. He knew that the road to winning depended on his ability to build up his endurance. That took years of strength training and of perfecting technique. Training—bike riding, playing soccer, hiking, even lifting weights, running through the woods, roller skiing, and learning how to ski properly—was fun. He learned that cross-country skiing involved natural movements. He learned to ski smoothly, with flexibility, and to keep both sides of his body even, not "kicking" harder on one side than on the other.

One could say that Tim Caldwell's childhood was not much different from the childhood of a boy growing up in Scandinavia. To become a great cross-country racer he had everything going for him. He participated in prep school races, then in divisional championships, and wherever he went, he did well. He had a strong base to build on, and he had decided that he would go on racing just as long as he enjoyed it and was improving. "If during two or three years I do not improve," he said, "I will retire. There is no sense to bang your head against the wall. You cannot go on if you are always two or three minutes off the winner's time in a 15-kilometer race."

In 1971, when he was but sixteen years old, he came to Scandinavia, where at Lahti, Finland, he placed fifteenth in the 15-kilometer race for juniors. At the Olympic tryouts before Sapporo in 1972, he placed second in the national 10-kilometer race; but the Olympic Games proved a disappointment. Almost the entire U.S. cross-country team was sick with the flu and turned in performances far beneath their true capabilities.

By the winter of 1973, Tim Caldwell was six feet tall and weighed 165 pounds. He won the U.S. national 15-kilometer race by fifty seconds and galloped to victory in his leg of the relay. That day he really felt strong.

His hopes were set on being among the first ten at the European Junior Championships at Leningrad. In the first Scandinavian race at Falun, Sweden, Tim Caldwell placed sixteenth. He had a bad run, but "if I have a good one," he said, "I can pick up a minute or two. But I don't know if I'll have it." The following week at Leningrad he just made tenth place; but he was still two minutes behind the German sensation of the season, Georg Zipfel, who had also beaten the field at Falun.

Ten days later, at the prestigious Holmenkollen in Oslo, Caldwell had a great race. In the 15-kilometer junior event he charged up and down the hills like Sixten Jernberg and John Bower had done, to place second, once again behind Zipfel. Caldwell, however, was only 17.8 seconds back; and he was only eighteen years old, still growing and learning.

Caldwell may well be encouraged by the fact that ever since the Grenoble Olympic Games the ages of winning competitors, even in the longer distances, have diminished. At Sapporo in 1972, the average age of the top five finishers in the 15-kilometer race was twenty-three. In 1973, at the Holmenkollen, the 15- *and* 50-kilometer races were won by Juha Mieto of Finland. He was just twenty-three years old. In the marathon event, he beat the twenty-two-year-old Norwegian Oddvar Braa by two and a half minutes. With scientific training methods being applied all over the world, the age drop will continue. For Americans this may be fortunate. The average winning ages now are in the sophomore-to-senior U.S. college age group. In 1974 Caldwell will be a sophomore.

4

HIGH MOUNTAIN SKI TOURING

In November, the snow came down the mountains. Around 4,000 feet it stopped and fell as rain. By December, the rock spires of the Alps were plastered white and the branches of the pines and larches on their flanks hung heavy. At Christmas, the streams were covered over, and the boulders that had been washed down from the heights centuries ago were now but smooth, indistinguishable mounds. The woods were silent as if suffering under their burden. High up on the glaciers, the cold weather and falling snow had formed solid bridges over the crevases. The wind whirled snow around the peaks and off the crests of ridges, and snow was whipped up and down the high altitude roads nature had created thousands of years ago. Where there were sharp drops in the glaciers, blocks of ice as big as Swiss chalets had formed. Called seracs, they hung precipitously and on occasion broke off with a roar spewing debris for hundreds of feet along the icy strips. Aside from these occasional changes, the heights were as silent as the forests they dominated. The days of the new year were often gray and cold, the nights long.

On February 1, 1933, near Grenoble, France, a man skinned up an almost obliterated trail, pushing one ski in front of the other. He was short and wore a black beret pulled down over his ears. On his broad back he carried a huge pack to which were attached a pair of crampons for climbing on ice, an ice ax, and a yellow tent. Inside the pack, which weighed over forty pounds, was extra clothing, sunglasses, tool kit, maps, compass, altimeter, toilet articles, and enough food for eight days.

In 1933, skiing was a very different sport from what it is today. There were few ski lifts, few ski champions; people climbed on foot or with wooden skis with sealskins glued to their bottoms. They climbed all day to some summit or pass in order to have a one-hour run down through virgin powder. Steel edges had just been introduced, nylon clothing did not exist, and ski boots were low and fashioned of soft leather. In general, ski equipment was heavy and fragile. Skiing was a mixture of touring and downhill; and for those looking for more adventure, it was a challenge of man against nature, or the utilization of intelligence in the service of man working for freedom and joy.

February 1, 1933. The date has little significance unless you are a student of mountain literature. Léon Zwingelstein was climbing alone through the woods. The sun was out and he was happy. Finally, after years of waiting and struggling to make a go of it in ordinary life, he had broken out. He was on his way. He had left his one-room loft in gray Grenoble where he had saved the money and planned his route, where he had designed and built much of his equipment and trained himself physically and mentally for the trials ahead. Zwingelstein, or Zwing as the few friends he had called him, was on his way to the greatest alpine voyage of all time: from Grenoble, France, to Nice on the Mediterranean coast; from Nice up into southern Switzerland, a dip into Italy, and thence to Austria. The main stops in his route would be Nice, Chamonix, Zermatt, the Jungfrau, St. Moritz, Galthur, Austria, back to Switzerland via Davos, the Bernese Oberland, and finally to Chamonix. When he finished (if he did) no crowds would greet him, not a friend would meet him as he stepped off the train at Grenoble, no newspaper, magazine, or television reporter would sketch his portrait and recount his exploit to millions of readers and listeners, and no manufacturer would use his name to publicize a product. Zwing, outside the main current of life, was a purist in the best sense of the word. He did not want or seek reknown or money. He was after something far more intangible. He wanted to accomplish the longest trek on skis any man had ever attempted in the Alps. Twelve hundred and fifty miles—the distance from New York to Kansas City, Missouri—around or over the highest mountains in Europe; and most of the time he would be traveling alone.

To put it mildly, it took either a fool or an extraordinary person to attempt a trip such as this. People had been crossing the Alps in winter for centuries: Hannibal with his elephants, invaders with their troops, travelers of old seeking spice from the Orient or another life in strange cities. They choose the easiest routes, skirting around the peaks or climbing through relatively low passes, then hurrying down into safe valleys and back to civilization. Since the early 1900's, ski mountaineers after pleasure had made the high route traverse from Chamonix to Zermatt a popular affair. Hundreds of people made the trip each season. They stayed overnight in chains of huts well spread out along the route. But up until 1933, nobody had been audacious enough to attempt the long and perilous solo trek that Zwing had conceived. Why did he do it? If fame or money were not his goals, what was he after?

Life as he knew it in the city of Grenoble depressed him. An engineer by profession, a dreamer by inclination, he was a failure in business. The modest fortune he inherited from his parents gradually disappeared during his frequent periods of unemployment. Office work was not for him, nor a normal, stable existence either. Misfortune haunted him. As a soldier during World War I, his eyes had been injured and troubled him during much of his lifetime. The girl he loved married his best friend. He never recovered from that shock, and to compensate for it, he poured all his energies into his one passion—mountains. He started climbing the peaks around Grenoble and then moved to other sections of the French Alps. At first, he climbed with friends. Later on, after disappointments and accidents, he decided he was better off alone. What he sought was an affinity with nature, the sense of dependence on himself alone, and the exhilaration of mountain heights. He became a camper, and to get to the mountains in winter, he became a skier, though he never took a ski lesson in his life. In the mountains he was calm, physically and mentally master of himself and his equipment.

Saturday afternoons after work he would catch a bus and head out of the city. He would camp out, climb a peak the following day, and return that evening to the city. That was the rhythm which kept him going. He depended on no one but himself. He climbed in spring, summer, and fall, and when winter set in, he escaped into the mountains with his skis and his tent, comforted only by his inner resources and the beauties of nature. Zwing was a loner, a strange figure, an oddball driven by one passion. From his point of view, he had little to lose in the mountains and much to gain.

It would be easy to say that he wanted to prove something, but that would not be true. Like all awakened men, he had to satisfy that human need to fulfill himself. Mountain climbing and touring provided that. To a friend he wrote: "Many young people look on mountaineering as a sport and all that includes: Physical exhaustion and fast climbs at any price. I believe that the person who loves mountains as I do has other feelings. The higher one climbs, the soul climbs as well and separates itself from everything that is below, in order to fly into infinity, toward that ideal, toward that goal which escapes our understanding, toward God." These fundamentally religious sentiments explain what Zwing and many other people who go into the high mountains are looking for. Solitude, peace of mind, freedom, and the sense of accomplishment that comes only from having extended oneself to the limits. Mountain touring, where the real adversary is not nature or another competitor but oneself, provides this.

For months, Léon Zwingelstein prepared his journey with tremendous care. Since he would have to carry all of his equipment himself, weight was an important factor. The tent he constructed weighed but four pounds. He made himself a windproof parka with flaps to cover nose and mouth. He designed special climbing crampons that could not only be attached to his boots but to his skis as well. He took along a gasoline stove, rice, whole grains for soup, cheese, biscuits, nuts, and dried fruit. With maps he studied every aspect of his route in order to reduce to a minimum the possibility of human error. He could not afford to get lost. To test his orientation abilities, on weekends he went into the mountains around Grenoble and practiced using his maps, compass, and altimeter. But there always remained the question of how he would react in high mountains he had never seen before or on practically flat glaciers, in fog and wind and cold where he was a total stranger. Only time would provide an answer to this uncertainty.

Natural dangers such as avalanches, rock slides, wind, fog, snowstorms, and cold all would have to be contended with in time. You could not take a three-month trip in the Alps in winter and not run into periods of bad weather. He studied how avalanches occurred and decided that in crossing dangerous slopes he would unhitch his sack and loosen his ski bindings. That way, if the snow began to slide, he could free himself and maintain a chance of survival because, for Zwing, life, especially in the mountains, was dear. He wanted to succeed in his adventure, if only someday to climb again.

A lone skier crossing the Alps in the winter of 1933—the vast Alps of four countries, the valleys and peaks, the jagged ridges and treacherous glaciers, the high passes and rocky mountains. Not only would he be alone, but also no one would know where he was. A twisted ankle, a broken binding, a mistake in itinerary, a bad storm —all of these things could prove fatal. He had to be ready for everything. In those days a lone skier could count on no one to come and rescue him.

Besides the dangers, life in the high mountains also had its attractions. For Zwing, the light-dark forests, silver glaciers, high rock spires, the sun, solitude, and closeness to God were worth the risks. For that, this rare human being was prepared to put his life on the line.

Late in the afternoon of February 1, 1933, he arrived in an isolated mountain village. The peasants thought they were seeing an apparition. He appeared out of nowhere. The dogs barked and jumped all over him. Children threw snowballs and hid in fear behind stone walls. Superstitious people, they refused him even a hayloft to sleep in, not to mention a hot meal. Traveling in the mountains like this, alone, the big sack and the heavy skis! Imagine! For them, Zwingelstein was too far out of the ordinary. Léon Zwingelstein calmly set about putting up his tent on the outskirts of the village. He prepared his supper, crawled into his sleeping bag, and went to sleep.

Day after day he skinned up the trails and zigzagged across the steep pitches. When the snow was hard, he climbed on foot, hauling his skis on his back. And when the ice appeared, he slipped on his crampons and gingerly made his way up to some mountain saddle. There he rested for a few minutes, ate some nuts and raisins, drank from his canteen, collected his equipment, and skied down. Sometimes the snow was light powder; sometimes it was wind-blown; sometimes there was a heavy crust that made turning practically impossible. Still, he went on and on.

Snow, fog, and wind. Occasionally in some village a gendarme would ask questions. Who was he? Where was he going? What was in the huge pack? Zwing answered his questions and handed over his passport.

"From Grenoble?" asked the man of the law. Zwing nodded. "Where are you going?"

"Switzerland, Austria," Zwing calmly replied.

"All alone?"

"Alone." Shaking his head, the gendarme handed back the papers and walked off.

In the woods and mountains he saw ptarmigan, weasels, hares, rabbits, foxes, chamois, and an occasional skier. His maps often proved inaccurate, and he had to proceed on instinct. In France's Grange and Crouzette Passes he lost his way. Then he was caught in a windstorm, and his eyes, still sensitive from his war injury, began to smart. By the time he reached Nice, he was very tired but not demoralized. He ordered a new pair of boots and rested. For the adventurer, a thousand miles of beauty and danger remained.

On February 12 he left again, only to get caught in a windstorm. He returned to the valley. The following day the cold got to him, and he froze his left hand. On the fourteenth, he slipped on an icy slope and went shooting off into space for a hundred yards. Through a miracle, his fall was stopped by the crampons that were strapped onto his pack. He picked himself up, took a deep breath, pulled his beret tight over his ears, and went on.

When there was no village or farm along his route to provide shelter from the wind, he cut a platform in the ice or snow and set up his tent. He cooked his food and slept the sleep of the just. In the morning the water in his canteen was frozen solid, and his boots were so stiff that he could hardly pull them on. Because of the cold, he had trouble keeping his climbing skins glued to his skis.

Some days he climbed and skied as much as twenty miles in more than twelve hours of incredible effort. And while he climbed, he let his mind wander. Why did he ever set out on this tour? Why go from Nice to Austria? To find peace? Interior happiness? He was like a traveling monk, a crusader seeking the Holy Land. Time and again he asked himself why he could not be content, like other people, down in the safety of the valleys.

He reached Chamonix, France, on February 27 and rested for five days. A friend, who was going to accompany him to Zermatt, joined him. For the Chamonix-Zermatt high route they had fine weather: warm sunny days and cold nights. Near Zermatt the friend left, and Zwing, happy to be in the mountains and alone again, camped at the base of the Matterhorn. By now he felt very strong and confident.

The following day, disregarding the advice of local guides, Zwing left in a windstorm and tried to climb the 15,000-foot-high Mount Rose. He fell into crevases, froze his cheeks, ears, and hands. Many hours later, when he stumbled into a mountain shelter, he realized that he had been very lucky. His injuries were painful but not serious. He had been saved from disaster only by his fine physical condition, which had made it possible for him to reach the hut despite the storm. A bivouac on the glaciers might have done him in.

On April 3 he reached St. Moritz; on April 6 the Tyrol region of Austria; on April 9 Davos. He was shocked by the "civilization" in ski resorts, the well-dressed downhill-only skiers, and the luxury of the hotels. He took a week's rest in the Ginanzalp and then climbed summits in the Bernese Oberland before returning to Chamonix on May 1.

During his great tour, Léon Zwingelstein wore out two pair of boots, his clothing was tattered, and his tent faded by the elements. On one exceptional day, carrying his heavy pack, he climbed over 8,000 vertical feet and covered twelve miles. His ski tour was 1,250 miles long, 170 miles of which was on glaciers. He went through 23 mountain passes that were between 6,500 and 10,800 feet high and through 22 passes between 11,000 and 12,500 feet high. He traversed 50 glaciers, all of which represented a *vertical* altitude difference of more than 193,000 feet or more than 36 miles. On his own steam—alone!

When he got back to Grenoble, he was satisfied. To a friend he wrote: "For myself I realized during my three-month tour that the mountains are everything. I can even say that they are my only reason to live, the only place where I am really alive." A year later, Léon Zwingelstein and a friend were killed when they fell off the summit of the Pic d'Olan.

In Alpine and Nordic racing the adversaries are always the other racers, even though everyone is running against the clock. The purpose of the organizers of any race is not only to make sure that everyone gets out of the start on time and is given his correct timing at the finish, but also that the conditions under which the skiers race are as equal as possible. Before the race, competitiors strive to understand the mountain or trail they are racing on, the snow conditions they will meet, the equipment they will need, and what personal efforts must be produced to win. In ski touring, as Léon Zwingelstein proved, the first adversary is nature, but more formidable than that is oneself. To "beat" nature Zwing had to protect himself from inclement weather, he had to study carefully his itineraries, and he had to prepare himself physically for the trails ahead. His life was on the line, and, as he knew so well, the natural adversary in a solo tour such as his was without mercy. But whether he would "win" or not depended even more on his ability to conquer personal fears, to remain calm in the face of danger or accident. The fact that he succeeded in his audacious tour proves that he won—not medals, glory, money, or fame— but a deep personal reassurance of his worth as a human being.

We all don't have to take the risks that Zwing took. In forty years, many things have changed to make mountain touring far more civilized and pleasurable than it was in Zwingelstein's time. In the United States and throughout the Alps, Alpine clubs and ski federations have constructed many mountain huts and shelters. With experience and care the trails that lead to these huts can easily be followed. They generally contain bunk beds and blankets, and sometimes during peak holiday periods are staffed with a hut keeper. At those times, meals can be obtained. In any case, a stove is always available to cook on, and often there is dry wood. Thus, it is not necessary to carry a tent, and the amount of food one must pack can be minimized. Mountain maps have become precise and are easily obtainable. For those who lack the experience, mountain clubs offer group tours.

Ski tours of all kinds—from the very easy jaunts of a mile or two to overnight trips from valley to valley through some mountain pass to strenuous two-week treks into wilderness areas—are possible. You don't have to be a mountain tiger like Zwingelstein in order to go on them. You can use lighter, stronger equipment and travel in safety. Around Aspen, Colorado, and Jackson Hole, Wyoming, in the Pacific Northwest, and in many areas of the eastern United States, mountain clubs and the United States Ski Association will provide information about where you can tour in winter and springtime.

In general, three types of touring are available to the modern skier: cross-country touring or running on prepared tracks; middle-mountain touring; and touring in the high mountains. These, though, are artificial distinctions since equipment is determined by the desires of the tourers and the conditions most likely to be encountered.

For example, for cross-country running on prepared tracks the skier needs extremely light, narrow skis with clip bindings very similar to those used by cross-country racers. If you are just going out for a couple of hours in the woods and on the plateaus, you will not need a rucksack. A parka tied around the waist with a selection of ski waxes, a pair of sunglasses, and suntan cream kept in a pocket completes your equipment. But if you are staying overnight in a hut, you will want a small pack containing extra clothing, toilet articles, and so forth.

For middle mountain touring, where you are never on glaciers, light-weight cross-country equipment is most agreeable, although in some cases less practical. Downhill running, particularly in crust or heavy snow, can pose serious problems. Light-weight cross-country skis made of wood can break. The new metal and plastic models are a better choice. Or, if the snow conditions are not right, you can use middle-width touring skis with cable bindings or regular downhill skis equipped with touring bindings and climbing skins. But nowadays the tendency in all forms of touring is to minimize weight in order to maximize pleasure.

For high-mountain touring, particularly on glaciers, downhill skis mounted with climbing bindings and equipped to take skins are a necessity. Since these skis will often be carried on your back, they should be as light as possible. Nowadays, certain models of metalo-fiberglass skis are reasonably light and practically indestructible. High-mountain touring (sometimes called ski mountaineering) requires some of the same equipment as does high-mountain climbing; but a lot depends on where you are going and for how long. If your trip takes you onto steep, possibly icy pitches, crampons are a necessity. These are ten or twelve tooth braces that are strapped onto the soles of ski boots. In high-mountain touring they are indispensable for climbing by foot on ice, on very steep pitches, and/or where the snow is particularly slippery. They are also occasionally used by the tourer on ice-glazed rock. Climbing knives or Harscheisen attached to the sides of skis are extremely useful. These are jagged metal plates about eight inches long and two inches high that attach to the sides of each ski. They are particularly useful for traversing steep icy pitches and are often used in conjunction with skins. Good-quality climbing skins and an ice ax for every two members of the party are indispensable. Skins are strips of synthetic plush material attached to the bottom of skis. The nap of the skins grip the snow and allow the skier to climb relatively steep pitches without sliding backward. When sliding forward, the hairs lie flat, providing a smooth surface. In olden times, the skins of seals were used, which accounts for their present name.

Up until the 1940's, skins were either glued onto wooden ski bottoms for long uphill climbs or were strapped on. Nowadays there are clip or track systems available. A sturdy nylon rucksack to contain this equipment, extra clothing, and food must be carried by each member of the party. In addition, the group will need a climbing rope, altimeter, compass, maps, and first-aid supplies.

Nylon has pretty much taken the place of wool in high-mountain outer clothing. It is light, windproof, water resistant, and comfortable, and it packs into a small space. Wool mittens with nylon outers or down-filled mittens keep hands warm even under extreme conditions. A wool shirt and wool knickers with knee socks are warm and comfortable. Nylon knee-high climbing gaiters keep snow off and out of boots. Footwear must be flexible for climbing and sturdy enough to give you support during downhill runs. Leather boots equipped with vibram soles are still the best choice.

Finally, the high-mountain tourer must be in good physical condition. In Chamonix, in the French Alps where I live, thousands of tour skiers from all countries set out on tours lasting from one to fifteen days. To prepare for the big tours, they work themselves progressively into condition and get accustomed to their equipment at the same time. They take several short tours, beginning in the late autumn and continuing throughout the winter months. Before starting on the trek up Mont Blanc, Europe's highest peak, or the high route to Zermatt, they get used to skiing up to some lower mountain pass and skiing down with a heavy pack. Then they set off in groups of two or three with or without a guide. These days few high-mountain tour skiers in the Alps carry tents. The European hut system makes it possible to plan the day's tour so that you arrive each night in a warm cabin or mountain hotel.

In the Alps and in some areas in the United States, life in the huts is a welcome relief to the rigors of the day. Unlike Zwingelstein in the 1930's, you do not have to cut yourself off from all of society. People from many countries with similar goals find themselves together for a brief stay. The huts are filled with warmth, chatter about the events of the day, and plans for the days to come. The food tastes marvelously good, and the bunk beds, though hard, provide warmth and a well-worked-for comfort. If you are tired in the morning, you can stay on an extra day; or if the weather is doubtful, you had best remain where you are.

Nowadays, weather reports are readily available, and in the event of an accident, rescue services are rapid and efficient. Helicopters and glacier planes have revolutionized mountain rescue. Under normal conditions, a broken bone need not be a catastrophe. In the high mountains, a basic knowledge of first aid is necessary and remaining calm essential. A bad situation can often be rapidly rectified by getting to the nearest telephone or to a mountain hut where help is available. It should not be forgotten, however, that in the high mountains you are basically on your own. Someday, you may have to bivouac, and a knowledge of how to build a a snow cave or construct a lean-to may save your life. It is a good idea, as well, to practice using a compass, an altimeter, and contour maps in good weather. Finding your way to a hut in a storm will be your recompense.

Forty years after Léon Zwingelstein's epic journey, the well-conditioned modern skier can derive enormous pleasure from touring either in the high mountains or on forest trails. I have friends in Denver who go on twenty-mile tours with their ten-year-old children in wintertime, sleep overnight in one of the Ski Association cabins, and continue for another twenty miles the following day. They use light-weight skis. They have learned to *wedel* (make short, tight turns) with them in the powder snow, and climbing uphill with such light equipment takes a lot of the pain out of the sport. The only painful part of their trips is the return to the city.

More and more people are taking to touring in order to find relief from city life and all that encompasses. The desire to get back to basics, to experience nature as it is without the mechanical innovations of civilization, is at the heart of the motivation of the modern touring skier. In addition, a lot of fun can be had for little money. High-mountain touring, particularly in wilderness areas, is still an adventure. You have to work hard for your pleasure and give up some of the comforts you are used to; but in so doing, you will most likely experience some of the sensations of discovery. And part of that discovery is a recognition of your own abilities.

With more and more people going into the mountains and to the huts, with rescue services, ski lifts, and roads available, Léon Zwingelstein might well say that the mountains have become too civilized. In a way he may be right; the solitude of the mountains has to be protected. But the fact is that much of the pleasure still remains. The beauties of running free through the woods on skis, the pleasures of attaining a 12,000-foot-high pass on your own, the joys of a controlled run down through virgin powder, the sense of accomplishment when you find the hut rising in front of you out of the fog, the glories of the glaciers in the sunshine with their seracs and the high peaks all about are there for those who want them. Luckily, there is still plenty of room for the tourer who is seeking solitude, peace of mind, and the satisfactions that mountains provide so well.

5

FASTER, FARTHER, AND BETTER

The development of skiing can be characterized by the struggle to go faster and farther, which, in fact, involves better technique and equipment. Much of this development has been achieved by racers and touring skiers often working closely with coaches, manufacturers, and technicians. It also follows that what the elite of the sport were doing yesterday, those who ski for pleasure are doing today. The skis that were used, the clothes that were worn, the techniques that were employed have been handed down to the recreational skier. Then the styles change. Someone figures out a new way to turn, another person designs a pair of ski trousers made from a new, comfortable synthetic material, a ski company produces a limited number of skis with a base they think is faster. Eventually, all of these new products, if they prove successful and commercially feasible, appear on the market. The racers are the avant-guard testers, the living laboratory and showplace for the new and the different. What is good for the racers—amateur or professional—is good for the public. That's the idea anyway, even though a lot of people still like to keep their wooden skis and baggy trousers, not to be better skiers but to be different from the rest.

Skiing in all its forms is not a static sport. It is constantly changing. When Jean-Claude Killy, Bobby Cochran, or Mike Lafferty schuss into the finish area and look back up the hill, they are all attempting to reconstruct their race. Where did they make mistakes, where could they have cut a gate closer or rode a flatter ski? By turning higher could they have taken a lower series of gates better? If they had used a softer or shorter ski, could they have picked up time in the turns or on the flats?

The Alpine skier's race to go faster does not stop at the finish line. Back in the hotels there are discussions with coaches and technicians. Then there are films to be studied and conclusions to be drawn, which can be applied in the next race or the following year. In summer, skis, boots, poles, even clothing will be tested on high-speed courses in Chile, on the New Zealand glaciers, or in summer ski camps in the U.S. and Europe long before the regular training season even begins. New materials, new methods of construction, gadgets of all kinds are put to the test under race conditions when the pressure is off. Mistakes are made, rectified, and conclusions are drawn. That's the rational way because for a racer to change skis or boots during the height of the competition season can prove disastrous. Time is to be gained, not lost.

After the race, cross-country racers ask similar questions. Was the wax ideal or should I have used a "kicker" wax to help get me up the hills easier, even though that would have slowed down the descents? Should I have started so fast when, after five kilometers, I was dog tired and the other racers were passing me by—people I had beaten in other races? Should I have double-poled more often and sunk into a deeper tuck in the downhill stretches? If I did more interval training in the springtime and less distance running, would I be in better overall condition? Back in the hotels or training camps, coaches are present to give guidance, make suggestions, and work with racers in the struggle to improve. Races these days are won by tenths, even hundredths of seconds.

After a tour, the ski mountaineer is concerned about his itinerary and equipment. Would it have been easier to go through a different pass in order to have a better approach to the summit? Would short skis have made the climbing easier without sacrificing safety on the glacier? Would dehydrated or freeze-dried food have given me as much energy and pleasure as the standard foods that weighed more and took a lot of space in the pack, space which could have been used for other useful equipment? Could the design of my pack be improved so that it would not pull so hard on my shoulders and still not sit on my hips? Is there a better way of attaching skis to the pack when climbing on foot, or would it be possible to drag my skis behind me with a rope tied around my waist?

Whether they are occasional racers or not, most skiers are constantly asking basic questions about technique and equipment. True, most people are skiing for fun, for the joy of being in the out-of-doors, for good laughs, and for exercise. But at the same time each person can learn a great deal by watching crack ski racers or experienced touring skiers in action. When you watch these men and women, you are watching the best in the world, on the finest equipment that can be produced. You can learn new ways of skiing and of using your body to advantage. You can learn how to ski in all kinds of snow and weather conditions, all of which helps you to be a healthier, happier human being.

You can apply what you have learned by occasionally entering races. I say occasionally because most top racers will tell you that too much racing is a waste of time. When asked what advice she would give to young people interested in a racing career, Nancy Greene replied: "Get rid of high back boots, go to a lower, softer boot. You have to develop a feel for snow, and at a young age with stiff boots you cannot acquire that. You have to sacrifice winning a few junior races in order to win later on. Then you have to ski, ski, ski—be the first one on the hill and the last one off at night, and don't stop for lunch. Free ski—do not race too much. Racing wastes a lot of time when you could be skiing."

Bobby Cochran agrees but adds: "It's not important to ski perfectly, technically, all the time. . . . The important thing is to really ski a lot and just go fast. Kids are very aggressive naturally and should not be held back by questions of technique. Fire down the mountain. Run courses with aggressiveness. Don't worry about technique. When you get older, you can pick up the technical part. Much of it you will be doing naturally. A lot of kids get screwed up with their arms—the upper body is not quiet. But it is really difficult to teach someone who has been held back, to give him aggression later on. Once the basic things have been learned, like turning and control of skis, a kid can go all out."

If you lean toward cross-country racing, or even if you just want to get good enough at it to enjoy yourself more while running through the woods, you should do a minimum of training. Tim Caldwell believes that training does not have to be a chore at all. "Don't mimic poor skiers," he advises. "You have to like what you are doing in order to do it well." Personally, Caldwell dislikes lifting weights, but he does it anyway: "You get a good deal of satisfaction out of having done it, and afterwards you feel just great."

If you are interested in high-mountain touring, eventually getting up onto glaciers in the United States, Canada, and in Europe, then you should start by doing a lot of hiking with a pack. With each trip you improve your physical condition as well as your technique. As you take longer and longer trips, perhaps with camping gear for an overnight stay in a lean-to, a cabin, or even a snow cave, you learn a lot about your equipment and yourself. In winter and spring, progressively more difficult tours with skins can be made as you become proficient in the basic movements, in skiing with a heavy pack in all types of snow conditions. With some notions of first aid and the precautions that must be taken when touring in avalanche-prone areas, with a knowledge of map reading and orientation, then you are ready—perhaps not to attempt a *tour de force* like Léon Zwingelstein, but ready to go into the high mountains with a family member or friend and enjoy all there is to offer when you have gotten there under your own steam. With new touring materials—skis, boots, dehydrated high-energy foods— packs have become lighter. A lot of the hard work has been taken out of mountain touring and a lot of pleasure has been added.

Whatever forms of skiing are most attractive to you, it's a good idea to keep in mind that there is always more to learn about going farther, faster, and better. By applying racing and touring techniques and keeping up with the latest in equipment, a great deal more satisfaction can be obtained from skiing.